Inside the Beatles Family Tree

RICHARD A EDMUNDS

First Edition Published 2018

AR Heritage Publishing, Berkshire, U.K, SL3 8TZ

ISBN 978-1-999683-5-9

Printed in Great Britain

Contents

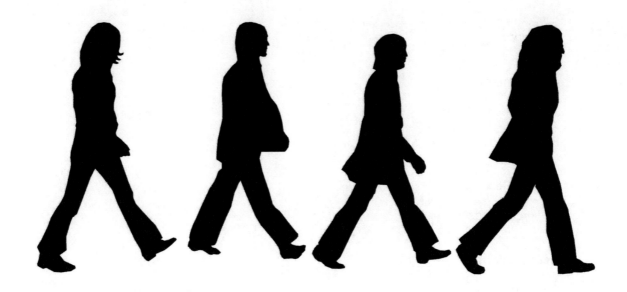

In memory of the late John Lennon and George Harrison any profits arising from the sale of this first edition will be donated to the National Foundation for Youth Music. This charity is in no way linked to the research, planning, finance or production of this work, and in no way endorses any statements or views contained within this work, which are entirely the author's own.

National Foundation for Youth Music
Registered charity No. 1075032.
9 Tanner St,
London,
SE1 3LE
020 7902 1060

Acknowledgements

I acknowledge and thank all those who have contributed to this project in any way, in particular Michael Byron of Liverpool for his prior online published research into the Lennon family, which was an invaluable template for the beginning of my own, John Lennon's second cousin Jean in Australia for her kind assistance with the Gildea family roots. Ringo Starr's cousin Janet Tranter for her help researching the Parkin and Starkey family roots, and for kindly agreeing for her own personal family photographs to be used in this work, and Catherine Pearson in Australia whose assistance in researching the military records of Charles Gildea was much appreciated.

I would also like to thank The Liverpool Record Office, The London Metropolitan Archives, The Public Record Office of Northern Ireland in Belfast, The Welsh National Library, Aberystwyth and The National Archives of Great Britain, Kew, for their assistance, and to thank all those who have generously contributed their photographic work or agreed for it to be used in this work. Every reasonable effort has been made to contact and credit the copyright owners of the images used in this publication, but if there are any errors or admissions, the publisher will be pleased to insert the appropriate credit and acknowledgments in any subsequent printing.

I would also like to thank, and to dedicate this book, to my friends and family for their support and patience during the long creation of this work.

Foreword

The city of Liverpool stands alone in the British Isles, unique in its vibrancy, diversity and strong community spirit. Founded in 1206 as a small port village, for many centuries it was largely insignificant and dwarfed locally by the more affluent nearby inland villages such as Walton on The Hill.

All this was to change rapidly in the 18th century when the construction of a dock complex catapulted the city's fortunes, placing it at the center of the Atlantic shipping routes, and attracting thousands of newcomers in search of work and fortunes. By the 19th century some 40% of the entire world's trade passed through Liverpool's docks and the city was the central point of contact between the old world and the new.

The various new communities that sprang up in the wake of this mass change were a vibrant patch work of different identities and cultures. Both the oldest African community and the oldest Chinese community anywhere in the British Isles can be found in Liverpool. As well as these relatively exotic newcomers, scores more were also attracted to the city confines from much nearer afield, Liverpool's long link with Ireland across the water of special importance, the city at times dubbed as England's *'Irish colony'*.

From this diverse melting pot sprang without doubt the city's most famous sons, four local lads, whose meteoric rise to fame in many ways mirrored that of the city that they hailed from. John, Paul, George, and Ringo, their names alone enough to identify them almost anywhere on the planet, from very ordinary beginnings achieved truly extraordinary heights.

Together as the Beatles they spearheaded what was to became known as the Merseybeat, a sound, attitude and movement, emerging on the banks of the River Mersey at the beginning of the 1960s, which would rapidly conquer the world with its simple, yet vibrant euphoria, catapulting them to an enduring super stardom, which in many ways continues unabated today.

The enormous fame surrounding the four Beatles has been such that almost every aspect of the band, their music, their lives, their loves, their immediate families and relationships has already been examined, and chronicled, in great detail, many times before.

It might then, indeed, be forgiven for thinking no scope remained for further works, yet it is a perhaps strange anomaly, that despite this intense scrutiny, the family roots of the four Beatles in the city of Liverpool have not, to date, received more than cursory attention.

The only previous stand-alone work dedicated to this area, *Up the Beatles Family Tree* a twelve-page work published in 1965, at the height of Beatlemania, remains the one serious, albeit brief, attempt to document the ancestral trail of all four Beatles. Individual Beatles biographers have tended to skim over their family roots as insignificant, or have instead filled the current vacuum of knowledge, by falling back on the scant earlier published accounts, inadequate though they are, and as a result, a variety of tales, more often than not belonging firmly to the arena of urban mythology rather than any serious academic research, have been told, and retold, time and again.

This work is my own attempt to redress some of that very real lack of knowledge of the family backgrounds of the Fab Four and wherever possible replace some of that existing fiction with real hard fact. I have resisted the temptation, wherever possible, to indulge in either speculation or assumption, or to fall into the trap of relying too heavily on existing unsubstantiated accounts, and family lore, but have instead began from scratch, researching the original documentary evidence in the archives, and the result of this, over several years, has allowed me to slowly but surely reconstruct their genealogy and history, both within the city of Liverpool, and further beyond.

As an experienced researcher, genealogist, author, and lifelong Beatle fan, this work is in many ways a merging of these personal passions. Whilst I have endeavoured and strived to make this book as factual and accurate as possible, I publish in the full knowledge that as with any history, be it national, local or family, further discoveries will doubtlessly come forward and add to the fuller picture, and possibly even alter it, in the future, as more records continually become available to the researcher, and are unearthed in previously unknown sources, and I therefore ask the reader in advance to forgive any such unintentional omissions or errors that might occur.

Readers will also notice that by far the greater portion of this work is dedicated to the ancestry of one band member, John Lennon. This reflects the fact that this project began as an examination of John's roots, only later growing to embrace his band mates too, and also reflects the fact that Lennon's family story has in the past, for various reasons, been by far the most open to wild speculation and urban *'myth making'*. The prominence given to John's ancestry therefore is indeed greater, but I wish to nevertheless make clear it is not intended to detract or take away from the equally important and interesting stories of his three fellow band mates contained within.

It is my sincere hope that this work proves as exciting and interesting to read, as it has been compiling, researching and writing.

Richard A Edmunds

January 2018

John Lennon

Few musicians have made such an indelible mark on the life and culture of the modern world as John Lennon. As part of the Beatles his music took the world by storm, reinventing popular culture, enthralling millions worldwide, and having an enormous influence beyond its humble origins in early 1960s working class Liverpool, which continues to extend to this day.

If an artist's works give a snapshot, however small, into the mind and soul of the creator, then it is undoubtedly by his simple and beautiful masterpiece *Imagine* John Lennon will forever be remembered. To some a hymn to assured atheism *'Imagine no heaven, no religion'*, to others a modern-day prayer for peace, an anthem for world unity, an enduring appeal to end man made divisions and war forever.

At heart however, John Lennon was less stable and self-assured in his outlook, if anything, the archetypal *'searcher'*, adopting new philosophies, spiritual paths, chemical stimulants, and musical styles, as others might adopt new clothes or hair styles, dropping them with equal speed, disillusioned as fast.

Perhaps the root to this stems from his difficult childhood. The 2009 film *Nowhere Boy*, gave a glimpse of this emotionally fraught period, when abandoned by his father, left with a mother with her own difficulties, he was largely bought up absent from both his parents, in the household of his aunt Mary *'Mimi'* Stanley and uncle George Smith. His relationship with his mother was all too briefly rekindled, before being tragically, and permanently, cut short by her death in a road accident outside his home when he was just 17, a monumental and devastating event for the young John Lennon. Father Fred would only ever sporadically reappear in his life, and then only once fame and fortune had come his way, with motives that were frequently unclear and at times perhaps questionable.

[1]

John Lennon, in Liverpool. aged eight, with his mother Julia Stanley

This early trauma had a defining influence on his life and his emotions, and ironically the complexity of character it created doubtless goes a great deal towards explains his unique talents. His songs are personal and empathetic. They touch the listener in a way few others do. Nowhere is this better displayed then in his haunting 1968 ballad to his late mother, containing the following lyric, inspired by the poet Kahlil Gibran; *'Half of what I say is meaningless, but I say it just to reach you..Julia'*.

One of the most intriguing periods of John Lennon's life and career came in 1972 when with his wife and partner Yoko Ono, he left England permanently for New York. Surrounded there by a large Irish-American community, traditionally and staunchly Irish Republican in their attitude and views, coincidentally the timing also ran parallel with the Bloody Sunday massacre in Derry, one of the most notorious events in the long-troubled history of Anglo-Irish relations.

Lennon drew on these new surroundings and influences, and his next album released just twelve months after *Imagine,* was as far removed, conceptually, from that earlier work as possible. The gentle and deep introspective philosophical musings of *Imagine*, now gave way to a new style, snappy, loud and brash, encapsulated in a cacophony of political protest song, and presented in the style of a typical American news stand daily.

Included in this work were two new compositions, that made his own feelings towards the Irish situation abundantly clear. The first *Luck of The Irish* included the following lyrics:

In the 'pool they told us the story how the English divided the land' [....] 'Why the hell are the English there anyway as they kill with god on their side? Blame it all on the kids and the I.R.A as the b*stards commit genocide.

This political rhetoric became even more embittered on the second track *Sunday Bloody Sunday*, directly inspired by the recent massacre, where Lennon not only criticised British troops, but controversially turned his attentions on the Loyalist communities of the North themselves.

You Anglo-pigs and Scotties, sent to colonize the North, you wave your bloody Union Jack and you know what it's worth. Repatriate to Britain all of those who call it home, keep Ireland for the Irish, not for London or for Rome.

The raw emotions roused by the massacre are understandable enough, a terrible event which is still a source of shame for the British government today, and Lennon's scathing condemnation of it is difficult to argue with, but the harsh overtones of sectarianism, and the overt nationalistic content, as contained in these lyrics, nevertheless sit uncomfortably with the same man who just twelve months previous had asked his listeners to *'Imagine no countries, nothing to kill or die for'*.

Around this time Lennon was publicly pictured with placards supporting the IRA, but his dalliance into the volatile arena of Irish politics would prove typically short lived. The distance began a year later, when Lennon reportedly refused to consider a free concert for Ireland's nationalists, without also playing a similar one for the loyalist community, perhaps suggesting he already regretted some of the harsher sentiment he had expressed towards them in music the year before. The following year, 1974, the IRA launched a campaign of violent terrorism on mainland Britain, including the targeting and murder of civilians, which was something Lennon could in no way square with his own inclination toward pacifist beliefs, and he distanced himself completely from any involvement with the IRA or in the troubles of Northern Ireland at this time. Some, including British ex-spy David Shayler, have claimed he continued to support the IRA financially, but this allegation has never been proved and would almost certainly have been noted in the abundant FBI covert surveillance documents on him, if true, so appears to be baseless.

Lennon marching in support of the IRA

Digital artwork based on a photograph by Rowland Scherman

Though his foray into Irish politics had now ended, almost as quick as it had begun, his personal interest in the land of Ireland and his own Irish roots continued. On the 1974 *Walls and Bridges* album art work he included a genealogical reference to the surname Lennon from the 1972 Dublin published scholarly work by heraldic expert Edward MacLysaght *Irish Families, their Names, Forms and Origins*. The entry concluded with the statement that no person with the name Lennon has ever distinguished himself in the field of culture or politics in either Ireland or England, beside which Lennon had added in his own handwriting, *"Oh yeh? John Lennon"*. The work was later belatedly updated with a reference to him!

In 1975 he gave his second son the name Sean, the Irish version of his own name, much to the displeasure of his stern aunt Mimi who had raised him. During this same period, he expressed the view that he considered himself more of an Irish musician than English and spoke of a sentimental desire to one day retire to the West of Ireland, though sadly of course this was not to be.

Perhaps this late adoption of an Irish identity was in a way a response to the total disconnection with this part of his genes and heritage. He had little to no contact with his father growing up, or any in depth knowledge of his paternal family origin. Shortly before his death in 1976 his estranged father Alfred 'Freddie' Lennon *(pictured inset)* sent through a manuscript to his son giving him the first detailed account of this heritage. Included in this was the now infamous tale that Fred's father Jack Lennon, the son of a ship's cook, had been born in Dublin, and toured America with a black and white minstrel troupe.

This story has gone on to be generally accepted, and much copied and repeated, despite no documentary evidence ever being brought forward to support it. Intriguingly Lennon's aunt Mimi, never a fan of Fred Lennon or his family, is on record in taped conversations sent to John in New York, dismissing the tale entirely as *'invented nonsense'*

Bill Harry, influential editor of the *Mersey Beat*, a long time personal friend and respected chronicler and historian of the Beatles, expressed his own doubts toward the accuracy of Freddie's account, largely based on conversations with Freddie's youngest brother, Charlie Lennon, who gave a rather different story. Charlie felt certain the Lennon family roots were actually to be found in Northern Ireland, though he too nevertheless believed the oft repeated American minstrel story to be accurate.

In 2006, Irish Folk Musician Michael Byron, an amateur genealogist from Liverpool, conducted his own research into Fred Lennon's family, which likewise found no evidence for the Minstrel story and proved beyond doubt that Fred's father Jack had in fact been born in Liverpool, not Dublin. In addition, he questioned the identity of Jack's parents, traditionally believed to be John Lennon, a ship's cook, and his wife, Elizabeth Morris. Through a thorough and detailed examination of the official census and BMD records Byron showed that this was undoubtedly incorrect.

This error seems to in fact have its origins in the first detailed family tree to be researched and published during the height of Beatlemania in 1965. The researcher in that instance, on finding the death certificate of Fred Lennon's father John '*Jack*' Lennon, had, working back from his age given on this document, 66, searched for a corresponding birth certificate for a John Lennon born in Liverpool in 1855, and found what he believed to be the correct listing. It was however not so, though Jack Lennon was indeed born in Liverpool 1855, and was baptised in the local Catholic chapel, his birth itself seems never to have been officially registered, not yet a legal requirement for families at that time. To be fair to the author of this sixties work, he was well aware of how tenuous this identification of Jack's parents was and made this clear, merely stating '*John Lennon, senior,* **may well have been** *the son of a ship's cook, also named Lennon, and his wife Elizabeth (Morris) of 65 Mulberry Street, Liverpool.*' Nevertheless, this went on to become accepted as a proven fact, including by members of the Lennon family themselves, and as a result has and continues to be copied, time and again, since.

My own research here on John Lennon's family history, whilst confirming much of the research of Michael Byron, will build upon it considerably. It aims to give for the first time an accurate and clear picture of John Lennon's roots, both paternal and maternal, to clear up many of the misconceptions that have come before, and cast an intriguing new light into Lennon's position in Liverpool's colourful patchwork of communities, his Irish heritage, and perhaps even, through this new perspective, reveal some of the root source of the conflict between the two sides of his family.

[4]

John Lennon's grandfather John *'Jack'* Lennon (1855-1921), right.
From *Charlie Lennon: Uncle to a Beatle* by Scott Wheeler, published 2005 by Outskirts Press.

The Lennons

Colourised photo of John Lennon, aged sixteen, performing with the Quarrymen, at St Peter's Church Fete, Woolton, 6th July 1957, the fateful day he met future Beatles bandmate, fifteen-year-old Paul McCartney.

What has never been in doubt, and is undeniably correct, is that Lennon is an Irish surname. The original source of the name being the Gaelic *Ó'Leannáin*. Anglicised into both *Lennan* and *Lennon* in Ireland after the Normans settled the land, the name was found spread across many parts of Ireland by the 16th Century. They were, perhaps unusually for the times, a notably peaceful sept, with little direct involvement in clan wars, and much involvement with the Irish Church, no less than six members of the family serving as *erenaghs* (keepers of holy places) at Lisgoole, near Enniskillen Ulster, in the 14th and 15th centuries.

The census records unfortunately do not survive for Ireland prior to 1901, so an exact idea of how numerous or widespread the family was before this date is not possible to know with certainty. However, the Griffith's Valuation of Land, taken for tax purposes in Ireland between 1848-1864, did survey every household in the land, and a close examination of this source shows that the surname Lennon was then concentrated in the Ulster province, most numerous in County Armagh (108 households), closely followed by neighbouring County Down (91 Households), both today in the modern state of Northern Ireland.

The first paper evidence of John Lennon's ancestors in England, comes in the year 1849, when on 29th April, his great-grandparents, James Lennon and Jane McConville, were married, at St. Anthony's Chapel, Scotland Road, Liverpool. At the time, this was the very heart of the Irish immigrant community in Liverpool, and would remain so for many years afterwards, and was consequently the only parliamentary constituency anywhere in England to ever return an Irish Home Rule M.P, T.P. O'Connor, to Westminster.

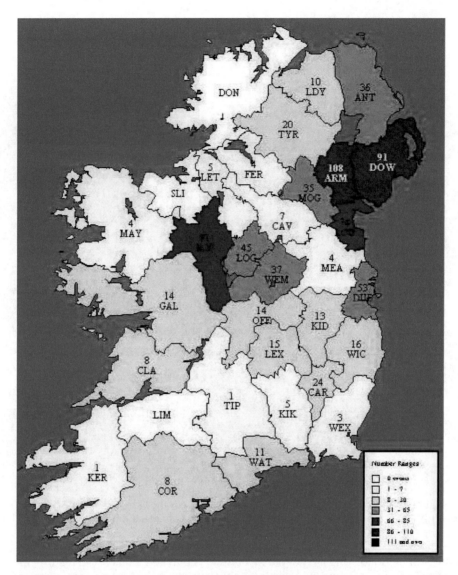

Distribution of the Lennon surname from Griffith's Valuation of Irish Land, 1846-50

The marriage was recorded in both the civil records, and the church records, and together they show James Lennon's address as Vauxhall Road, his parents recorded as Patrick Lennon, a farmer and his wife Elizabeth. Jane's address was given as Saltney Street, and her parents were given as James McConville, an engineer and his wife Bridget.

It is also at Saltney Street, that the couple are found living, two years later, on the first surviving census record for them, James Lennon was then recorded as twenty-two, a merchant warehouseman, and Jane as twenty, a housewife. With them was the first child to the marriage, a daughter Elizabeth, born eight months before in Liverpool. Both James and Jane confirm on this document that they were indeed part of the city's Irish immigrant community, together recording their birthplaces as Ireland.

As suggested on the marriage record, also living on this same street in 1851, a few doors along from the Lennon household, were Jane's parents, her father James McConville, forty-one, mother Bridget McConville, forty, and two younger brothers John and Richard McConville, seventeen and fourteen respectively, all of whom were likewise recorded as born in Ireland.

[7]

Marriage Register entry of John Lennon's great-grandparents James Lennon and Jane McConville,
April 29th 1849, St Anthony's Roman Catholic Church, Liverpool.
Liverpool Record Office, ref no 282 ANT/2/1

Though these 1851 census records do not elaborate as to where in Ireland either the Lennons or McConvilles originally came from, fortunately later census records for them do provide this information. Two decades on, in 1871, James Lennon, by then widowed, recorded his birth place as County Down, as did his mother-in-law Bridget McConville, also by then widowed and living with her son-in-law and grandchildren, within the Lennon household.

Though Jane McConville/Lennon had come to England with her parents, it seems unlikely that James' own parents, Patrick and Elizabeth Lennon, ever left County Down, as no record can be found placing them in Liverpool. As a farmer, Patrick Lennon should in theory appear on an earlier tax record, the Irish Land Tithes taken in County Down 1826-1834, and they do indeed contain the record of four Patrick Lennon's, one in Ballyphilip, one in Aghaderg, two in Drumgath.

Had it been possible to find a baptism for James Lennon in the Irish church records it may have been possible to narrow down which, if any, of those four, was his father. The documents in Liverpool make it clear James Lennon was born around the year 1829, but unfortunately the surviving Roman Catholic parish records through Ireland at this early date are fragmentary and far from complete and, despite searching, it has not proved possible, to date, to further identify the Lennon family origins there.

Jane McConville's roots in Ireland, and County Down, however, can be traced with much greater certainty, and exactly pinpointed to the town of Newry, evidenced by her baptism there on the 8th of May 1831, at the town's Catholic Cathedral. Her baptism does not record her mother Bridget's maiden name, however her younger brother John's baptism, two and a half years later, on 27th October 1833, in the same chapel, does, where it is given as Torley, like Lennon another anglicised version of an ancient Gaelic sept name *Mac Toridhealbhaigh* roughly translated as *'son of the image of the towering warrior'*.

The same Griffiths Tax Valuation records which show the Lennons predominately located in Ulster, also shows the McConvilles and Torleys predominately located at the same time in Newry, with no less than sixteenTorley households and twenty-two McConvilles liable for tax payment there. Interestingly four Lennon households are also recorded in the town, with at least one, on Castle Street, with both Torleys and McConvilles recorded as immediate neighbours, so it is tempting to suggest that James Lennons' family may also have been from Newry, and rather than travel alone, he travelled with his future wife and her family to Liverpool, but with the concrete evidence only a baptism could provide, sadly lacking, this must remain speculation.

As to why the Lennons and McConvilles left County Down for Liverpool, some time before 1849, again we are firmly in the realm of speculation, devoid of any firsthand account from the families themselves, but given the wider historical setting, we are perhaps on a much firmer footing to posit the likely reason.

The years 1846-9 were the very height of Irish emigration into Liverpool, a direct result of the unfolding catastrophe across the water in Ireland, in the deadly grip of *an Gorta Mór,* the 'Great Hunger', the worst natural disaster to ever hit the country.

Newry, Co. Down, Ulster, Ireland, 1902.

This momentous and calamitous event began as a widespread blight on the potato crop across Europe, in the winter of 1845, likely first bought in on ships from the Americas where two successive year's crops of potatoes had been destroyed by blight in 1843 and 1844.Though this was not the first time the potato crop had failed in Ireland, it had in fact done so twenty four times in the proceeding one hundred and seventeen years, a variety of factors conspired to turn this occasion from a mild hardship, as it had so often been before, into a national and humanitarian disaster of unparalleled proportions, a dire catastrophe forever etched into the collective memory and consciousness of a people.

Chief amongst these was the peculiar historic and economic development of Ireland, and its resultant status as a virtual colony within the United Kingdom, which had seen the majority of the population, the Catholics, barred from owning land by law, and pushed into subsistence farming on leased small hold plots, subdivided within family units into even smaller plots over time, and often held by absentee and disinterested British landlords.

As a result, the potato, a new world crop that could be grown easily, abundantly, and on tiny parcels of land had become the staple food for at least a third, and the poorest third at that, of Ireland's population, a situation replicated nowhere else in Europe, leaving Ireland particularly vulnerable to the worst effects of the blight when it came.

The famine also had unfortunate timing, coinciding with the height of the belief in free market economics in London, which argued against intervention in the free flow of the market, even on humanitarian circumstances. The absurdity, and sheer inhumanity of this, is displayed by the fact that Irish exports, of other foods and livestock, unaffected by blight, actually increased during the famine. The sight of food leaving by boat for sale in the towns of England and Scotland, often by necessity under armed guard, while the native Irish starved in millions, was something never to be forgotten amongst the populace, and later provided the source of much fertile propaganda for Ireland's flowering young nationalist movement.

The combination of both these factors could have been, nevertheless, survivable, had it not been for the third and most deadly factor to compound this latest blight, and this was the simple fact that it did not go away as it had before, but rather repeated itself, inflicting continued suffering for four successive winters.

[9]

Though most survived the initial blight of winter 1845, and the famine in its wake, with the British government aiding the stricken by stockpiling and distributing cheap Indian maize, they had been considerably weakened nonetheless and were in no state to survive a second, let alone a third and fourth onslaught of dire hunger. In their weakened state disease rapidly took hold, and deadly maladies, particularly typhus, began to ravage the land.

At the same time an untimely change of government in England, saw attitudes harden at precisely the worse moment, one incoming Member of Parliament. famously responding to Ireland's dire

Women harvesting the potato crop in Ireland 1900

plight with *'once is unfortunate, twice your own folly'*. Instead of food aid being freely distributed, harsh constraints were instead placed on it, with the poor and starving expected to work on public road works, to earn their relief, with the predictable result of starving and skeletal men dying, shovel in hand, trying desperately, in spite of their condition, to feed themselves and their families.

In total it is estimated that near to one million persons perished in the Irish famine, and at least a million more emigrated, depopulating the land massively to this day. Many of those who were able went to America, but the vast majority, too poor to afford the long passage across the Atlantic, instead followed the trail of the food exports, making the short hop across the Irish sea to the sister nations of Scotland and England, where poverty and hunger was by no means unknown, but where the poor were at least not generally suffered to die in the streets as in Ireland, and plentiful work could still be found in the mills and factories of the growing urban industrial powerhouses, Dundee, Glasgow, Manchester, and London.

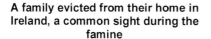

A family evicted from their home in Ireland, a common sight during the famine

A contemporary depiction of the suffering caused by the famine
London Illustrated News 1847

Liverpool, however, received by far more emigrants from the famine than anywhere else in the British Isles, being just a short distance across the sea from both Belfast and Dublin, and the traditional first destination for those leaving both places. Even before the famine, around 18% of Liverpudlians who responded to the 1841 census, gave Ireland as their birthplace. Though not the largest Irish diaspora in Britain, which was to be found in London, Liverpool was nevertheless far and away the city with the highest proportion of Irish in relation to their overall population.

The increase of Irish coming into Liverpool on the outbreak of famine, turned from an ever-growing trickle in the first year, to a veritable flood of distressed humanity by the second. A report from the Christmas Day 1846 edition of the *Liverpool Mercury* tells of a special meeting convened by the Liverpool select vestry, responsible for the poor relief of the parish, to take into consideration the *'recent enormous increase of Irish paupers to the town'*.

The result was a letter drafted to the Home Secretary in which they complained that the *'Irish paupers coming into the parish of Liverpool had increased to a most alarming extent in the last six weeks'*, with the figure for the week ending December 19th reaching 13,741. In comparison the corresponding figure for the same week the previous year had been just 888. They estimated that nine tenths of the paupers fleeing Ireland were coming first to Liverpool, and pleaded for special consideration of their parish's *'peculiar position'* as first port of call for the refugees, and pressed the need for urgent government action to help the town cope with the pressure now bearing down upon it.

A week later the same paper reported that the offices of the parish relief authorities in Fenwick street *'were besieged with applicants'* 15,400 soup tickets and 800 bread rations handed out in the first four days of the new year alone. The first letter to the Home Secretary evidently met with no reply, and the edition for the newspaper published on 29th January 1847 reported a renewed and urgent plea by the same select vestry, to Westminster, drafted in a tone by now heavy with desperation, the numbers presenting for poor relief having reached a truly staggering 130,795 applicants a week. To put this into context the entire population of Liverpool recorded on the 1841 census was barely 241,000, so this represented a sudden increase of more than half the town's normal population.

Irish Emigrants preparing to leave their homeland in the hope of finding salvation across the sea.

Though this probably represents the peak of the emigration, new refugees continued to come, with an estimated quarter of a million people travelling from Ireland to Liverpool in just 1847 alone. The initially sympathetic reaction from locals soon turned sour, as the burden of paying the upkeep for such a huge influx of destitute unfortunates began to be reflected in raised rates, and successive waves of typhus and cholera, began inevitably, to spread out from the Irish and into the host populace. In November 1847, the tone of the *Liverpool Mercury* was noticeably different from the winter before, an editorial asking its readers *'as to the poor Irish who make Liverpool their home. When will there be an end to this work?"* The diatribe goes on to describe them as a *'plague, an evil, and an intolerable nuisance, [...] both from spreading disease [...] and by their great numbers reducing the local populace to an even worse condition then their forced bounty.'*

Though many of the Irish immigrants undoubtedly moved on again, to America, or returned home after the famine, Liverpool was forever changed, a further newspaper report of 1849 stating that now at least one in four inhabitants of Liverpool were Irish born, a figure backed up two years later by the 1851 census.

No shipping records between the ports of Ireland and England exist to pinpoint exactly when the Lennons and McConvilles might have come over. In all likelihood, it was on one of the paddle steamers that regularly travelled the trade routes between the two Island's great ports, many of the proprietors of these shamelessly cashing in on the misery in Ireland, extending their business from freight to human cargo, cramming hundreds at a time onto their unsanitary and unsuitable open decks. This practise was condemned roundly, though somewhat belatedly, in an investigation towards the end of the famine, in April 1849, by a Captain Denham, who found in one week alone over 4,000 had been transported into Liverpool as deck passengers, packed together in conditions which even the men carrying them lamented as *'most painful'* pleading *'for the sake of humanity, [let] something be done'.*

Denham described scenes he had witnessed at the port of Liverpool as *'sickening and distressing, [...] a loathsome spectacle'*, including women and children crammed into filthy pens meant for horses, and pregnant women forced to give birth in busy engine rooms. He witnessed a total of three deaths from deck exposure that week, two women and a baby. Despite the conditions, most passengers did manage to survive, though he nevertheless thought this a part of the problem, precisely because this served to encourage a misplaced complacency towards the practice, *'a collective forgetting that human endurance can reach a fearful height without actual dying.'*

Liverpool's memorial to the Irish Famine, St Luke's Churchyard

In Denham's 1849 report, he mentioned that the three worse offending ports sending paupers to Liverpool, in such a manner, were Dublin, Drogheda and Newry. As early as October 1846 the *Liverpool Mercury* was reporting deaths in Newry from starvation. In February 1847, at the height of the famine, the same paper reports that the Reverend J.D Smith of Newry addressed the George Street Chapel in Liverpool, giving *'an appalling account of the misery and destitution caused by the famine in his land and advocating at great length the claim of the Irish people for British support, a collection being made at the close of his address for the Irish Mission'.*

That there existed a regular traffic of famine refugees from Newry, at the time John Lennon's ancestors left that town for Liverpool, is also attested to by a report from the *Liverpool Mercury* 1849 on the wreckage of the vessel *Hannah* just outside Quebec, carrying 149 men, women and children, mostly agricultural workers, and all paupers from Newry, over half of which were killed when the vessel hit an iceberg, the master and several of his crew shamefully abandoning ship with the only life boat, leaving their unfortunate human cargo to meet a grim fate in the freezing waters.

A steamer on the Newry Canal, at the turn of the century.

[13]

Advert for the *Sea Nymph*, placed in the *Liverpool Mercury* July 1846, a steamer which travelled, twice weekly, between the ports of Newry and Liverpool, carrying freight and cargo.

Advert for the same steamer just ten months later, having now extended its business to human cargo, the desperate able to buy a place in steerage for just five shillings. Many landlords gladly paid this fee to remove the poor from their lands, rather than be burdened with the greater responsibility and cost of their upkeep.

Perhaps ultimately the exact circumstance of the Lennon and McConville family's arrival into Liverpool will never be known with certainty, but as to the new life they found for themselves once there, this can be said to have been only marginally better than the one left behind.

The huge influx of destitute souls, crammed together into the city's poorest quarters, inevitably led to an increase in crime, more than doubling in the decade during and immediately after the famine. Despite the Irish comprising a quarter of the population, more than half those arrested came from this populace, a fact which did not endear them to their new neighbours. One contemporary commentator noted that the new Irish seemed to *'prefer the certainty of an English cell'* to the horror of being returned back to their homeland, a real possibility if they were deemed a drain on the parish rates, through poor relief. This, of course, in itself explains why so many were driven in the first place toward a life of petty crime to survive, rather than take the risk of appealing to these same authorities for aid.

In spite of this tough and unforgiving environment, into which the Lennons and McConvilles now found themselves thrust, the records show both James Lennon and his father-in-law settled down immediately to building an honest and decent life for their families, in their new home at Saltney Street, directly opposite the Liverpool Docks. James found work as a Warehouseman, and occasionally when he could, worked as a Cooper, a skilled trade, which suggests he had been apprenticed and trained in Ireland before the famine. Father-in-law, James McConville, took menial jobs as a Day Labourer when and wherever he could, despite the fact he too had been a skilled workman in Ireland, a trained Engineer.

Saltney Street, Liverpool home to the Lennons and McConvilles after arriving from Ireland in the 1840s. James Lennon perhaps found first employment in these imposing Victorian tobacco warehouses.
Photo John S Turner

As evidenced by the 1851 census James and Jane Lennon's first child, a daughter Elizabeth, had been born to them not long after their marriage in the July of 1850. A second child came another two years on, a son named James for his father, born in the August of 1852. However, it was to be the couple's third child born to them in Liverpool, a second son, born on 12th of January 1855, and baptised two days later, at St Nicholas Roman Catholic Chapel, Copperas Hill, Liverpool, that was to become the grandfather to Beatle John Lennon. Also originally christened as John Lennon, perhaps for his maternal uncle John McConville, despite this the child himself would always be known affectionately within his family as '*Jack*'.

Baptism of John Lennon's grandfather, John *'Jack'* Lennon, January 14th 1855, from the register of St Nicholas Roman Catholic Chapel, Copperas Hill, Liverpool.
Liverpool Record Office Reference Number: 282 NIC/1/4

By the time of the 1861 census, young '*Jack*' Lennon and his family had moved to No.3 Paget Street, Liverpool, a mere half a mile from their old home in Saltney Street, where two more boys had been born into his family, William George Lennon, in 1858, and Richard Francis Lennon, in 1860. James Lennon was again recorded on that year's census working as a Warehouseman and Cooper, and wife Jane Lennon's mother Bridget Torley/McConville, had now also come to live with them, her husband James McConville having died shortly before, leaving her a widow at just fifty.

Eighteen months on from this census another son was born, Patrick Lennon, doubtless named for his paternal grandfather back in Ireland, followed another two years later, by the couple's seventh child, Joseph Lennon born in January 1865, exactly a week before older brother Jack Lennon's tenth birthday.

[15]

Road, Street, &c., and No. or Name of House	HOUSES		Name and Surname of each Person	Relation to Head of Family	Condition	Age of		Rank, Profession, or Occupation	Where Born
	Inhabited	Uninhabited (U.), or building (B.)				Males	Females		
3 Paget Street	1		James Lennon	Head	Mar	3_		Warehouseman Cooper	Ireland
			Jane do	Wife			29		do
			Elizabeth do	daur			16	Scholar	Lancashire Lpool
			James do	Son		8		do	do
			John do	Son		6		do	do
			William G do	Son		3			do
			Richard do	Son		1mo			do
			Bridget McComill	Mother in law	Wid		57	Formerly Servant	Ireland do

1861 Census, John Lennon's grandfather Jack, aged six, living at 3 Paget Street, Scotland Road District, Liverpool. *Crown Copyright, ref Class: RG 9; Piece: 2657; Folio: 122; Page: 58; GSU roll: 543007*

The happy family unit they had built in their new home was sadly not long lasting, the following year, 1866, the Lennons, now living in Eldon Place, Liverpool, being hit by a double blow, when in April son Patrick died aged three and a half, followed only weeks later by his sister, the oldest child to James and Jane, and their only daughter, Elizabeth, who tragically died right on the cusp of adult life, just two months short of her sixteenth birthday. How this affected the family, and in particular, Jack Lennon's mother Jane can only be guessed at. Pregnant at the time, she gave birth to the couple's final son Edward Lennon, seven months later on 31st January 1867. Whether the recent traumas had left her weakened or not, just two years on she herself died at the family home, in childbirth with their ninth child, a daughter also sadly not to survive, on January 29th 1869, at just thirty-seven years of age.

The 1871 census finds the family, in the wake of this tragedy, still at Eldon Place, James Lennon, who would never remarry, recorded as widowed, living with five of his six surviving sons, and, again, his mother-in-law Bridget. Jack Lennon who had turned fourteen shortly before his mother's death, was now sixteen and recorded working as a Railway Clerk. His elder brother James, eighteen, was working in the local warehouses, like their father. Missing from the family home however was younger brother William Lennon, who then aged thirteen, had been sent away to Theological College, and would later follow this calling, becoming a Roman Catholic Priest.

St Joseph's Roman Catholic Church, Blundellsands, Crosby, Lancashire. On completing his training, Jack Lennon's younger brother William was first appointed chaplain of Birkdale Farm Boys Reformatory School, before becoming priest of the newly built St Joseph's, twelve miles north of Liverpool, in 1886. He remained there two decades and was well thought of in his community. *Photo Sue Adair*

[16]

Another four years on from the 1871 census the first of James Lennon's sons, eldest James Lennon, junior, was married at St Francis Xavier Roman Catholic Church, Liverpool, to his bride Ellen Ford. Perhaps to ease the burden on his father, he took his grandmother Bridget with him into his new marital home, where she would remain until her death in 1882, at the age of seventy-one.

The next census, taken in 1881, records James Lennon, senior, aged forty-eight, again employed as a Warehouseman, with his younger sons Richard, twenty, and Edward, fourteen, lodging in a room over a Provisions shop at Pownall Square, Liverpool. Jack Lennon, who would have been twenty-six at this time had clearly moved out from the family home, though curiously it has proved impossible to find him anywhere on the census records this year. This in fact means from his appearance on the 1871 census aged sixteen, until the time of his own marriage in Liverpool, in August 1888, at the age of thirty-three, there is a sixteen-year gap in the known records of the life of John Lennon's grandfather.

This raises the possibility that he did indeed travel to America as a young man, the family tale which has been so often repeated in the various previous examinations of John Lennon's ancestry. Certainly living in such close proximity to the docks, with ships regularly departing for the U.S.A just a short distance away from his home, he would have had plenty of opportunity, if inclined to do so, though it seems questionable as to whether he could have been married whilst there, as the tale also insists, his 1888 marriage in Liverpool, at least, recording him still as a bachelor at that point.

West Waterloo Docks Liverpool, where American packet ships berthed. Millions of people, more than any other port in England or Europe, left from here on their voyage to the New World.

His older brother James Lennon, junior, died prematurely, a year after the wedding, at Jack's home in West Derby, so it is possible Jack Lennon had been abroad and his brothers' dire illness around this time had precipitated a sudden return home, with Jack later deciding to stay and marry, though this is only speculation and it is just as likely he was never overseas at all.

Another aspect of this family story regarding John Lennon's grandfather, one of the most enduring tales, some would argue myth, that has since passed into folklore, and which has already been briefly touched upon in the introduction to this piece, is the belief he spent at least part of his time in America touring as a refined minstrel in the performing troupe *Andrew Roberton's Kentucky Minstrels*. This tale, which at least two of his sons Alfred and Charles Lennon believed, deserves further and closer examination, precisely because it has been so widely accepted and reproduced by many other authors in print, despite an apparent lack of any outside evidence to support it. This has led some at the other extreme to dismiss it as entirely fabricated. The very existence of the troupe has been called into question, as no trace of such a performing outfit ever touring America has, to date, been found.

My own research has shown this dismissal is over hasty, the troupe itself was real enough, and further still it did indeed have links with Liverpool.

The origin of the troupe lay with Andrew Roberton, a Scotsman and Music Hall entrepreneur, from Edinburgh, who began his career as a performer, and later manager, of *Birrell's Diorama*, a Victorian mobile variety troupe, which had first formed in 1873. Part of Birrell's act had consisted of a minstrel show, the *Royal Scottish Caledonian Minstrels*, and it may well have been this that gave Roberton the idea to branch out on his own, when in the early spring of 1891 he moved with his family to Bradford, in the north of England, and teamed up with a Phillip R. James. Together the pair began advertising for performers for a new act they labeled *James and Roberton's Original Boston Minstrels*.

The pair's *Boston Minstrels* toured for a short while in South Wales, with some success, but both the act and partnership were to prove short lived, Roberton announcing publicly in the newspapers that he had severed all ties with James and the troupe they had formed together, a mere six months later, returning in haste, with his family, back to Scotland.

Andrew Roberton *from a portrait in the Cardiff Mail, February 14ᵗʰ 1898*

Whatever the reason behind this, it does not appear to have long dampened Roberton's own desire to run a successful Minstrel troupe and he soon busied himself in Scotland with the necessary preparations to start up in business again, this time on his own, placing an advert for performers in the London newspaper *The Era* on December 19ᵗʰ of the same year, reading as follows;

Wanted, clever coloured ladies and gentlemen and first-class Minstrel talent in all lines, stump orators, knockabouts, musical turns, novelties, specialties, good interlocutors, soprano, contralto, tenor, baritone, bass vocalists, harp, cornet, bass, flute, trombone, drummer, limelight and baggage men. For a long tour to commence 28 Jan 1892. Report three days previous for rehearsals. All must be thoroughly competent, strictly sober, and dress well on and off stage. To save time and unnecessary correspondence, give full detailed particulars and lowest terms for long and comfortable engagement. Address, 4 Clerk Street, Edinburgh. Should like to hear from Major Carr, Frank Broom, Robert Jackson, Charles Carey and George Tichner.

[18]

A minstrel show put on for the ladies of the Bethnal Green Workhouse, a charitable act by local bankers and 'respectable' gentlemen who had 'blacked up' for the evening, safe in the knowledge they would be unlikely to encounter any of the poor unfortunates in their day to day lives.
London Illustrated News 1868

This gives some idea of the varied flavour of the act he now set in motion forming, and in this manner, through local newspaper advertisements, Roberton sourced his talent from the towns and cities of the U.K. He christened this new company, consisting of both white and black performers, *Andrew Roberton's American-European Original Kentucky Minstrels*, though, like the Boston Minstrels before, there was in fact nothing remotely American about Roberton's music hall troupe at all, apart from the fact that like all British *'Refined Minstrel'* acts, it mimicked a style which had its origin in the American Negro Minstrel shows that had previously toured Britain in the 1830s-1870s, in the latter period, often comprising of genuine newly freed slaves, being contemporary with the period of the American Civil War and black emancipation in the United States.

Roberton's new company, which was firmly in the booming British Music Hall tradition, was unusually large by the day's standards, 30 *artistes* in all, and made its stage debut, a week after he'd initially hoped, in early February 1892, like the *Boston Minstrels* before them, in the familiar music halls of South Wales. Evidently a great believer in the power of self-publicity, he celebrated the opening night by placing no less than ten separate adverts in the same edition of one London newspaper declaring his company '*An unprecedented, gigantic success, artistically and financially, the cleverest and most respectable company of ladies and gentlemen ever seen!'*

Four weeks later he placed yet another ad letting it be known his company continued to enjoy immense success, and their audiences in Swansea were '*packed to suffocation nightly'!* How much of this was huff and bluster can only be guessed at, but contemporary reviews certainly seem to suggest they were genuinely popular speaking of *'crowded audiences'*, and *'warm receptions'*, frequently using expressive adjectives such as *'highly enjoyable'*, *'strong performances'*, *'a capital show!'"*. One such reviewer from 1892 describes the program in quite splendid detail:

[Roberton's Minstrels] *are thoroughly entertaining, comprising many new and melodious selections of minstrel song, comic verse and choruses, with fine falsetto singing, clever and amusing burlesque of scenes from operas, high class selections by the band, a ludicrous stump speech and other items all equally mirth provoking.*

Among the performers listed as regularly performing with the troupe were:

Kool Kennedy, Harry Matthews and Dock Watson, Negro comedians, the Kentucky Choir of Negro Minstrel Song, Frank Broom, Charles White and Fred Adams, eccentric dancers and acrobatic specialists, J.J Dykes' Orchestral Band, Arthur Elliston, Male Soprano, Henry Lloyd, tenor vocalist, The Musical Lindsays, experts on several instruments, Lewis and Chip Chase the 'Frisco Tornados, comedians and tap boot dancers, the Comical Ivies, the Liliputian Wonders, The Burlesque Zouaves, the Two Monetas, and Mr. Robert Saphrini, the Burlesque Prima Donna!

[19]

Within a year this weird and wonderful act had proved so successful they had undertaken three tours up and down the country and been commissioned for a further tour, across the water in Ireland.

In 1893 Roberton branched out into partnership with Walter Holmes, a fellow showbiz impresario, together opening their own music hall venue, the People's Palace, in Bradford, Roberton's adopted home town in England. As part of the deal Holmes also gained a share in the existing troupe, and it was thereafter altered in title to *Roberton's and Holmes Coloured Operatic Kentucky Minstrels.* However like his previous attempt at partnership, this would again be fraught with tension, and lasted barely two years before ending in an acrimonious split in the April of 1895, which would see Holmes drag Roberton through the courts for damages, and blacken his name in several national newspapers.

In the wake of this the troupe became simply *Andrew Roberton's Kentucky Minstrels* and would thereafter remain so. However it was still under the former name *Roberton's and Holmes Coloured Operatic Kentucky Minstrels,* that the company made its first ever appearance in Liverpool on Monday February 18th 1895, at the zenith of its popularity, beginning a fortnight residence at St. James's Hall, Lime Street.

Liverpool Mercury 18th February 1895.
(Note the Liverpool Police also had a rival minstrel act!)

It is possible that the forty-year-old Jack Lennon went to see them perform in Lime Street at this time. Contemporary newspapers report them as being very well received in the city and drawing consistently large sell-out audiences whilst there. However, this was not their only visit, and the troupe returned to Liverpool, for a longer month-long stint, just over two years later, in the summer of 1897, this time taking residence at the *Tivoli Palace*, the hottest new venue in the city, opened a year before, in a fanfare of publicity, with Music Hall's biggest star, Marie Lloyd, as the headline act.

As in all the towns and cities where they performed, Roberton, ever the master of publicity and showmanship, had his troupe parade loudly through the city streets each morning before a show, in a colourful and exotic '*Silver Mace Drill Parade*', which could hardly have been missed by any who happened to view it, and must have drawn a throng of amazed and enthralled onlookers, even in such a cosmopolitan dock city as Liverpool.

[20]

Perhaps significantly, during this second residence in Liverpool, Roberton advertised in the city newspapers for new musicians to join the troupe. Maybe significant too, immediately following this tour of Liverpool, the troupe moved on, in early August 1897, to Dublin for a brief engagement there. It is possible Jack Lennon did answer this advert, found employment with them at this time and, subsequently, went on the tour with them to Dublin. This may then have been later skewed in the telling into the more familiar tale which later came down through his family, and saw him instead coming from Dublin and then touring America with the Kentucky Minstrels. Such jumbling and confusion of exact detail, over the long passage of time, is a common aspect of orally transmitted family history and tradition, but of course tempting as this theory is, it must remain speculation only.

WANTED, Double-Handed Musicians, to Augment Orchestra. Long and Comfortable Engagement to Competent and Sober Men. Others save stamps. Full particulars, references, and lowest terms to ANDREW ROBERTON, Kentucky Minstrels, Tivoli Palace, Liverpool.

Advert placed July 10th 1897 during the troupe's tour of Liverpool. If true Jack Lennon did join, then it was possibly in response to this ad.

Roberton's Minstrels themselves continued to tour for another two years after they last played Liverpool, though their popularity had by now begun to wane with changing fashions. Not least amongst these was the embryonic growth of the cinema with silent moving pictures, which Roberton himself had been amongst the very first entrepreneurs to pioneer in the U.K, introducing this new medium to excited audiences at his Bradford Music Hall venue as early as 1896. It was obvious this was now where the future lay for the savvy businessman and in this brave new world, live acts, such as the Minstrels, were rapidly becoming yesterday's news. The turn of the century would see their eventual demise, with the winter tour of 1899-1900 being their last.

What is certain is that throughout their nine-year career, during the height of the British Music Hall era, they enjoyed great success and travelled extensively all over England, Wales, Scotland and Ireland. What is equally clear is though Roberton initially promoted them as *direct from America* there is no evidence that the show ever toured there. Their movements are very well documented, and an extrovert showman such as Roberton, would have been unlikely not to have boasted, and boasted loudly at that, in detail of such a high-profile engagement, so it appears highly unlikely they ever did.

Similarly, to date, there lacks still any independent evidence to support the claim that John *'Jack'* Lennon was ever a member of their troupe. Certainly, all the documentary sources that do exist for him at the relevant time consistently record his occupation as a Freight Clerk. Though the above links with Liverpool perhaps shows it was not entirely beyond the realm of possibility either, it may indeed have been just a tall tale, an embellishment, from a man who had seen the spectacle of them marching through his home town, and wished his own amateur music career, knocking out a tune or two in the local public house on a weekday night, had reached similar dizzying and respectable heights. Unaware of the even greater heights of success his grandson would one day scale, he would doubtless, in any case, have never expected such a claim to receive the intense and close scrutiny it since has!

For now, on this, the jury must then, unfortunately, remain out, and we return to what are the known and provable facts in regard the life of John *'Jack'* Lennon. These as they stand, provide no clue either to the possible American sojourn, or an American first wife, and since his children also believed this wife had died in childbirth, it seems likely they were in fact referring to Margaret Cowley, the wife he married in Liverpool on the 19th August 1888. The existent documents show, Margaret then twenty-two, eleven years her husband's junior, was not an American, but very much a native Scouser, the daughter of John Cowley, a Liverpool Engineer.

[21]

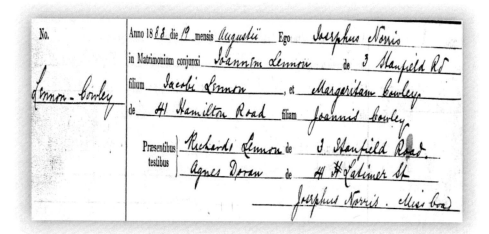

Marriage of John Lennon's grandfather '*Jack*' Lennon to first wife, Margaret Cowley, recorded in Latin, in the register of the Roman Catholic Chapel of the Immaculate Conception, Everton. His address 3 Stansfield Street, hers 4 Hamilton Road, both in the Everton district.
Liverpool Record Office Ref 282 IMM/2/2

Witnessing the wedding was Jack's younger brother Richard Lennon, and on the civil document Jack recorded his own occupation, not as a Musician or a Performer, but a Book Keeper, and his father James's occupation as a Car Owner. This information matches the 1891 census records where Jack's father, James Lennon, is found living at 373 Walton Breck Road, Walton On the Hill, Liverpool, with his youngest son Edward Lennon, twenty-four, and his family.

James, then aged sixty, had indeed changed occupation, no longer working in the local warehouses, as he had ever since coming to Liverpool from Ireland, now instead describing himself as a Tram Car Company Manager. Perhaps he had saved his money over the years, to invest in his own business, and certainly the heavy physical labour environment of the dock warehouses, would not have suited many men long into old age. Though exact detail of the company he ran is not known, certainly this would likely have referred to a horse drawn carriage rather than any sort of motorised tram, or vehicle, which were still, at that point in time, a good few years off from coming into general usage.

Horse drawn tram on the streets of Lime Street, Liverpool 1890s, at the same time John Lennon's great-grandfather James owned and operated a tram car company there.
Liverpool Record Office

[22]

Returning to his son Jack Lennon, he and his wife Margaret were recorded that same year 1891, with their first child, daughter Mary Elizabeth Lennon, aged two, lodging at 63 Allen Street, Warrington, Lancashire. Jack Lennon, now thirty-six, again recorded his occupation as *'Railway Clerk'*, the same occupation he had given on the last census he had appeared on twenty years previous, in Liverpool, at the age of sixteen, again not really suggestive of any great dramatic change of career path on his part.

Interestingly however, this document did record his birthplace, not as Liverpool, but as Dublin, which is not correct, but may suggest he was a man in the habit of not always telling the exact truth in regard the details of his life, and this may have been the source of his son Alfred's later confusion on this point.

Alternatively, and equally possible, the form was likely filled out by the head of the house they were lodging in, and he may simply have guessed his place of birth. As a man raised in an Irish household by two Irish parents, Jack would likely have had a noticeable Irish accent, and certainly on no other record he himself filled out does he ever again give Dublin, or anywhere other than the correct place, Liverpool, as his city of birth, which might lend this latter, more generous theory greater support.

John *'Jack'* Lennon, with his first wife Margaret and daughter Mary, lodging at the household of Warrington joiner Richard Holloway, April 1891. *Crown Copyright, Class: RG12; Piece: 3076; Folio: 97; Page: 36.*

The year after this census was taken, Jack Lennon's family life was hit by tragedy when Margaret Lennon died giving birth to their second child, a son, named Michael. Sadly, he later died too, just two and a half weeks after his unfortunate mother, at the Lennon family home in Rose Vale, Everton.

Understandably devastated by this sudden turn of event, Jack Lennon is said to have forever after kept a portrait of his first wife in pride of place in whichever home he was staying, keeping her memory dear and close to him always for the remainder of his own life.

Despite his deep grief, the practical challenges of being a Victorian working man, alone with a four-year-old daughter to support, soon became abundantly clear, and a pressing concern, and Jack wasted no time in advertising for a live-in housekeeper to help him cope. This position was filled by twenty-one-year-old local, Mary Maguire. Born and raised just a few streets away from Jack Lennon's home, in the neighbouring Liverpool district of West Derby, the young Mary was a bright and vivacious girl, universally known to her family and friends as *'Polly'*.

Though a native Scouser, like Jack Lennon, at least part of her own roots lay in Ireland. Her father James Maguire, a horse keeper and general labourer, had been born around the year 1840, to an Irish Catholic family in the small village of Whitewood, in Nobber, County Meath, some fifty miles to the north of Ireland's capital Dublin. Originally the site of a Norman Castle and Moat, and pronounced as *an Obair* in Gaelic, coincidentally, given the later musical success of Polly's grandson, this rural town was also the birthplace to one of Ireland's most celebrated musicians, the blind itinerant fiddler Turlough O' Carolan.

[23]

Turlough O' Carolan (1670 – 25th March 1738)

Born in the wake of Oliver Cromwell's conquest of Ireland, and living through the momentous years of the Boyne, Turlough is considered the last great composer of traditional Gaelic music, and Ireland's national composer. Travelling the land with his harp, he composed over two hundred and twenty songs, and weddings and funerals were often delayed until he could arrive to perform. Though he later settled with his wife, Mary Maguire, in County Leitrim, he was born in Nobber, County Meath, also birthplace to John Lennon's great-grandfather James Maguire one hundred and seventy years later, giving this small rural corner of Ireland a double musical claim to fame.

MAIN ST.NOBBER.CO.MEATH.8646.W.L.

**Nobber,
Co. Meath,
Ireland,
original home
to the
Maguire
family**

Like the Lennons, it would appear the Maguires left their Irish home in the wake of the Great Famine. The Protestant Church tithes imposed upon the Irish Catholic population, recorded the Maguires, in 1826, living on a small plot of just less than seven acres, five of which were poor for farming, precisely the kind of holding which fared worse when the great calamity hit the land two decades later. Accordingly, James' parents Roger and Bridget Maguire headed to Liverpool, with James and his two younger sisters, when they were still just small children, sometime between the years 1846 and 1851.

On arrival they settled in Liverpool's Old Swan district, and for a time made their home there in Queen Street. Later rechristened in the early 20th century as Macqueen Street, the death certificate of James's mother Bridget Maguire from November 1867 shows members of the family were occupying at least two homes there at that time, at numbers four and eight.

A mere two months on, a forty-five-year-old widow, Ann Hargreaves, gave this street as her address on her remarriage to another Queen Street resident, quarry man, Edward Rowlands. This lady was the great-great-grandmother of Beatle George Harrison, and in fact not long afterwards, in 1871, her daughter and son-in-law, stone mason Edward Harrison, would also join her there, living just a few doors along from the Maguire family, first at number fourteen, later number twelve, and that couple's children would thereafter call the street home for over half a century, with most their children, including George Harrison's grandfather Harry Harrison born and raised there.

The coincidence does not, however, end there. The 1911 census records the very same house where John Lennon's great-great grandmother had died forty-two years previously, number four Macqueen Street, in the occupation of Harry's twenty-four-year-old brother George Harrison. Both brothers would sadly die in the Great War not long after. Harry's son, Harold, twelve at the time of his uncle George's death, two decades later named his own youngest son, Beatle George Harrison, in memory of him, an eerie little coincidence, giving this small otherwise entirely insignificant little row of houses a double *'claim to fame'* in the wider Beatles story.

[25]

Macqueen Street, Old Swan, West Derby, Victorian home to both the Maguire and Harrison families.

By the time of Bridget Maguire's death, her eldest daughter Mary had been married for three years, and her youngest Catherine was to marry shortly after. James's himself had not married, but had begun a lasting relationship with a local Liverpool born dressmaker, Mary Porteous, Polly being the first child born to the couple in the November of 1871. Four more children would be born to them, Catherine in 1873, James in 1874, William in 1876, and Ellen in 1878.

The 1881 census records Polly, her siblings and mother, living in Whiteford Street, West Derby, father James away for the home, perhaps working, and their elderly widowed grandfather, Roger Maguire, seventy, temporarily filling his place as the man of the house.

Baptism of Mary _'Polly'_ Maguire/Mcguire, John Lennon's grandmother, St Michael's Roman Catholic Church, Liverpool, 1871. _Liverpool Record Office, Ref. 282 MIC/1/1_

Mirroring the experience of the Lennons, tragedy was also to strike the Maguire household with the death of Polly's mother Mary the year after the census, at just thirty-six years of age. The eleven-year-old Polly, left to cope with the task of looking after her younger siblings while her father went out to work and support them, was now forced to grow up quick. James Maguire, John Lennon's great-grandfather, meanwhile seems to have suffered a slow decline after his wife's death. By 1901 he was recorded living down and out in a crowded Doss House for men, and by 1911 his fortunes had sunk even lower, and he was an inmate at the West Derby Union Workhouse in Belmont Road.

The Belmont Road Workhouse, West Derby Liverpool, where John Lennon's great-grandfather, Irishman James Maguire, ended his days as a pauper.

This grim institution was opened in 1891 as a *'Test House'* catering primarily for the able-bodied poor and vagrant offering them day relief in return for manual labour. This consisted primarily of breaking rocks, an arduous task more commonly associated with prisoners, and indeed, prison awaited for any '*inmates*' who refused to carry out this task to the full satisfaction of the workhouse board of guardians, as evidenced by the case of forty four year old inmate John Brown, who in 1897 was put before them having, exhausted, refused his overseers orders to break *'any more stones that day'* and was promptly arrested and sent to prison for fourteen days as punishment.

Despite occasional concerts and dramatic plays put on to raise moral of the men and women, an 1895 report on the workhouse, which often contained as many as eight hundred souls crammed within its walls, described the atmosphere as *'oppressive'*, and the inmates as *'dispirited and listless'*. Often the men and women who found themselves there were driven to extreme distress by their experience, such as the out of work *'Negro Comedian'* who after ill treatment by the institution in 1893 returned and threw a brick through their window, or the far more extreme case, the same year, of forty four year old Thomas Roberts, who, having been admitted unable to earn his living because of crippling ulcers to his legs, deliberately plunged three stories to his death from the workhouse windows in despair. James Maguire would certainly not have entered such a place unless in very dire need himself and bereft of all other alternatives.

Meanwhile his children, as soon as they were old enough, had all been put out to work. The 1891 census shows Polly lodging in a local household with brother James and sister Ellen. Polly's occupation was recorded as a Laundress, whilst fifteen-year-old James was an Office Boy at the docks, and thirteen-year-old Ellen was a General Domestic Servant.

It was eighteen months after this census that Polly, still only twenty one herself, but already well used to the role of surrogate mother from the bitter experiences her short life had dealt her, responded to widower Jack Lennon's appeal for household help for himself and his daughter, and, once living in his home, despite the sixteen year age gap that existed between them, the pair grew close, their relationship rapidly developing from a strictly professional arrangement, into that of a lasting romantic attachment.

[27]

Mary 'Polly' Maguire, with her younger siblings James and Ellen, boarding in the household of Owen Connolly, a Cork Cutter, at 40 Lombard Street, West Derby, Liverpool, 1891 Census.
Crown Copyright Class: RG12; Piece: 2997; Folio: 128; Page: 24

When Polly fell pregnant with their first child the following year they moved together into new lodgings, almost opposite to her childhood home, in Bourne Street, West Derby, and here, in the September of 1894, she gave birth to a son, named John for his father. He sadly contracted diarrhea and died at just over a year of age, an all too common cause of Infant mortality in Victorian era Britain, especially amongst the unsanitary living conditions which was the general lot for the majority of the working classes.

Two further sons were soon born to the couple in various different short hold rents in the immediate surrounding streets of West Derby, Walter Lennon in the November of 1896, and John Arthur Lennon born a year later in November 1897. In early 1898 the family moved yet again, this time taking Jack's now retired father, James Lennon, along with them, to Caradoc Road, Seaforth.

Their tenure there would prove to be a terrible one. Eldest son Walter, not long after, developed a gum infection whilst teething. In a time before penicillin this was an extremely dangerous complication for a child, and having spread to his lungs, it led to the loss of his young life at just eighteen months old. Only three weeks on from this latest family tragedy Jack's father James Lennon also passed away, in his case succumbing to kidney disease at the age of sixty-nine.

Polly's younger sister, Catherine Maguire, temporarily moved into the family home to help the devastated couple cope with their remaining children, Jack's daughter Mary, now nine, and younger son, John Arthur, but tragically just a month later the youngest followed both his older brother and grandfather, dying aged just eight months, like the couple's first son and his namesake John, another victim to infantile diarrhea.

The suffering of Jack Lennon, who had similarly endured the rapid deaths in succession of his sister, brother, and mother some twenty years previously, can hardly be conceived of, and doubtless both Polly and Jack wished to leave this home, where over just a few short months dire ill-fortune had so viscously plagued them, as soon as was possible, rapidly moving on again before the year was out, from Seaforth in the far north of the city, to Toxteth in the south, where they would thereafter remain.

Shortly after the move Polly fell pregnant again, giving birth nine months on, in the March of 1899, to the first daughter to be born to the couple, whom they named Catherine Lennon, in gratitude to the newborn's young auntie who had been so helpful during their recent troubles. Sadly, their dreadful ill luck seems to have followed them, and she too, was born sickly, and passed away at just four days old.

[28]

Caradoc Road, Seaforth, Liverpool, home of Jack and Polly Lennon in 1898, and last home of Jack's father, John Lennon's Irish immigrant great-grandfather, James Lennon (1829-1898).

Another daughter Beatrice came along a year later in May 1900, but history again repeated itself, contracting meningitis during Christmas week, tragically she passed away two days into the new year of 1901, at just seven months of age.

With all five of the couples' first children dying in infancy, unusual even by the standards of the day, Jack and Polly, both raised as Catholics, now took to unusual, perhaps desperate measures, choosing to take their children to St Joseph's Protestant church, some four miles away from their home, where all of their next nine children were instead baptised. Perhaps comments had been made in their local Catholic congregation about the unmarried status of the couple. Despite both being quite free to, they did not wed until nearly two decades into their relationship in 1915. As a result, they may have feared this dreadful run of infant death was some sort of awful divine punishment. Perhaps, just as likely and understandably, it was a move made out of sheer distress, desperation and superstition.

Whatever the case the couples dire fortune, and bitter familial tragedy, continued unabated in the same vain, both of their first two children baptised in the Protestant tradition, William Lennon, in January 1902, and Joseph Lennon, in March 1904, also passing away, William at eight months of age, like brother Walter before him of complications whilst teething, Joseph at five months old, yet another victim of the terrible epidemic of infantile diarrhea. Both were buried, back at the local Catholic cemetery, in the family plot, alongside their unfortunate elder siblings.

[29]

John Lennon's grandparents, Jack and Polly Lennon, with one of their fourteen children, which it is not known, but the clothes seem to date from the mid-1890s.

[30]

It was not until the eighth child born to the couple in the August of 1905 at the then family home, 28 Denton Street, Toxteth, a son George, that Jack and Polly Lennon's union was at long last blessed with a child that would go on to survive, prosper and grow into adulthood.

Denton Street, Toxteth home of the Lennon family 1904-06.
Liverpool Record Office

He was followed by two more brothers Herbert Lennon, on 18th April 1908, and Sydney Lennon, on 26th July 1909, both of whom would also thrive and prosper, Sydney living to the grand age of ninety-three, the last of John Lennon's uncles to die, in his adopted home Canada, in 2003. By this time the family had moved again, a short distance, into 27 Copperfield Street, which they would affectionately refer to as *'Coppie'*, This would be the Lennon family home for the next four decades, and here they were found living on the census of April 1911, Jack Lennon again recorded, as ever, as a Freight and Shipping Clerk at the dock warehouses.

The Christmas before yet another son had been born to them, Harold, and he is recorded with the family that year, aged five months. Sadly, that summer, he would become the eighth of the couple's children lost to childhood illness, yet another victim of epidemic diarrhea, though thankfully this latest tragedy would prove to be the very last the already greatly overburdened Jack and Polly would be forced to endure.

A year on from baby Harold's death, on 14th December 1912, the twelfth child of the couple was born. Another son, he was christened Alfred Lennon, and known to his family as *'Alf'* or *'Freddie'*. He too was initially sickly as a child, contracting the bone disease rickets, necessitating the fitting of a metal leg brace which would seriously stunt his early growth. Again the likely cause was the poor diet and malnutrition the family faced as a result of their living conditions, but unlike his unfortunate siblings before him, this child, John Lennon's father, thankfully survived, and was soon followed by a further two siblings, younger sister Edith, Jack and Polly's only surviving daughter, in February 1915, and youngest brother, Charles *'Charlie'* Lennon, the fourteenth and last child, born exactly a fortnight to the day after the end of the First World War, and five days after Polly Lennon's forty seventh birthday, in late November 1918.

Polly, described by Freddie Lennon in his own biography as a mother he idolised, a witty, sharp woman who never, visibly, let the tragic blows life had repeatedly dealt her, get her down, may have been forgiven for thinking life had at last turned a corner for them, with six healthy and happy children finally bringing a much-needed breath of life and energy to the family home.

Sadly, this was to prove an all too brief period of joy and stability, with the family once again plunged into turmoil, when in 1921, at just fifty years of age, Polly was widowed, husband Jack Lennon dying in the family home of liver disease, aged sixty-six.

[31]

Freddie Lennon, still only eight years old himself, recalled being taken up by his mother, to the bedroom in Copperfield Street, to view the body laid out, with large copper pennies placed over the eyes, in the traditional Irish manner, and being told to say his last sad goodbyes to his father.

Polly Lennon now faced an unenviable uphill struggle to raise her six children. The eldest, George, turned sixteen just eleven days after his father's death, and was therefore old enough to fend for himself, as were, to a lesser extent brothers, Herbert, thirteen, and Sydney, twelve, in an age when working full time at such young ages was by no means uncommon, particularly in working class areas such as Toxteth. Eight-year-old Freddie, six-year-old Edith, and two-and-a-half-year-old Charlie, presented more of a problem, and unable to cope for long, Polly applied to the local parish for charity relief. The result was an offer to take Fred and Edith, both of school age, into the local Bluecoat School for Orphans, whilst she would be left to concentrate her efforts on clothing and feeding the youngest child, Charlie, perhaps with what little help her eldest sons could provide her from their combined wages.

Mary *'Polly'* Lennon, nee Maguire (1871-1949)
John Lennon's indomitable grandmother.

With little other realistic option, and painfully aware how injurious poverty could be to the health of vulnerable young children, she understandably jumped at this offer, and Fred and Edith were promptly sent off there for the remainder of their schooling years, only returning briefly to their family home, mother and siblings, during the school holidays. Harsh though this move may seem, it was in fact far from a cruelty, if anything the high standard of education offered by the Bluecoat School, a prestigious and respected institute, was far beyond what most working class children of Fred and Edith Lennon's peers could either expect or hope for, offering each of them a golden opportunity to better their social standing and break free of their cycle of poverty, with Edith Lennon eventually doing so, going on to carve out a good career for herself as a school teacher.

Blue Coat School for orphans, Wavertree, Liverpool, where Fred Lennon and sister Edith were educated after death of their father in 1921.
Photo Sue Adair

The young Fred Lennon however, was not similarly inclined to a life of scholarship and academia, and when he eventually left the school, after spending six years there, aged fifteen, he instead found his first paid employment working as a Bell Boy at Liverpool's Adelphi Hotel. For a time after he seems to have taken a variety of menial work, causing elder brother Sydney to lament his apparent reckless and willful intent to waste all his *'good education'*.

In 1930, at the age of seventeen, he took the first tentative steps towards a life at sea, when he joined the crew of the *Montrose* for a month long posting as a ship hand. A further two years on, in the spring of 1932, aged nineteen, he took the plunge fully, and signed up for his first long term posting, a nine months engagement as *'Ship's Boy'* aboard the steam turbine passenger ship *Duchess of Bedford*.

However around the same time, shortly before first setting sail on the seas, an even greater life changing event was to occur, when on a somewhat cold and drizzly Sunday morning outing with friends in Liverpool's Sefton Park, dressed to impress in clothes a size too big for him, loaned from long suffering brother Sydney, an attractive red haired girl who caught his eye, fifteen year old Julia Stanley, and as a result of this chance meeting, the course of the young Freddie Lennon's life would change forever.

Bluecoat School Uniform, Circa 1925.
Photo Albert Blundell

[33]

John Lennon's father Alfred '*Freddy*' Lennon, in his ship's stewards uniform, holding up his crew number, taken at twenty-six years of age, in 1938, the year he married Julia Stanley.

Naval rating card of John Lennon's father Alfred Lennon (1912-76).

Crown Copyright, held at National Archives, Kew, series BT349

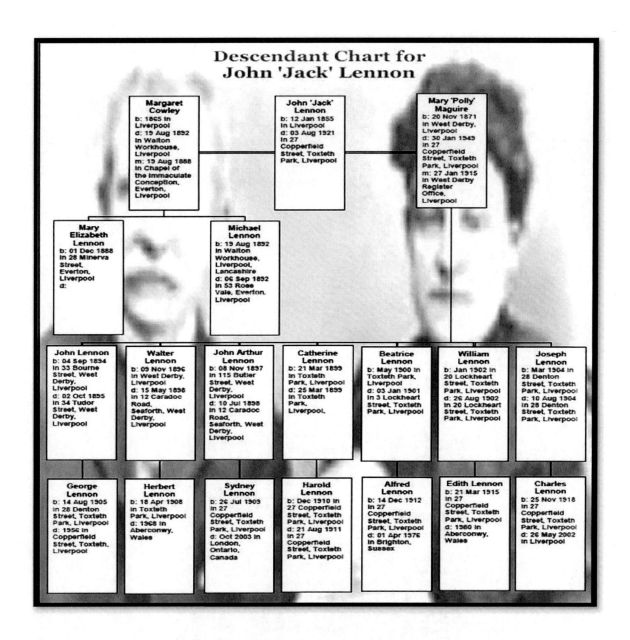

Descendant Chart for John 'Jack' Lennon

Margaret Cowley
b: 1865 in Liverpool
d: 19 Aug 1892 in Walton Workhouse, Liverpool
m: 15 Aug 1888 in Chapel of the Immaculate Conception, Everton, Liverpool

John 'Jack' Lennon
b: 12 Jan 1855 in Liverpool
d: 03 Aug 1921 in 27 Copperfield Street, Toxteth Park, Liverpool

Mary 'Polly' Maguire
b: 20 Nov 1871 in West Derby, Liverpool
d: 30 Jan 1949 in 27 Copperfield Street, Toxteth Park, Liverpool
m: 27 Jan 1915 in West Derby Register Office, Liverpool

Mary Elizabeth Lennon
b: 01 Dec 1888 in 28 Minerva Street, Everton, Liverpool
d:

Michael Lennon
b: 19 Aug 1892 in Walton Workhouse, Liverpool, Lancashire
d: 06 Sep 1892 in 53 Rose Vale, Everton, Liverpool

John Lennon
b: 04 Sep 1894 in 33 Bourne Street, West Derby, Liverpool
d: 02 Oct 1895 in 34 Tudor Street, West Derby, Liverpool

Walter Lennon
b: 09 Nov 1896 in West Derby, Liverpool
d: 15 May 1898 in 12 Caradoc Road, Seaforth, West Derby, Liverpool

John Arthur Lennon
b: 08 Nov 1897 in 115 Butler Street, West Derby, Liverpool
d: 10 Jul 1898 in 12 Caradoc Road, Seaforth, West Derby, Liverpool

Catherine Lennon
b: 21 Mar 1899 in Toxteth Park, Liverpool
d: 25 Mar 1899 in Toxteth Park, Liverpool.

Beatrice Lennon
b: May 1900 in Toxteth Park, Liverpool
d: 03 Jan 1901 in 3 Lockheart Street, Toxteth Park, Liverpool

William Lennon
b: Jan 1902 in 20 Lockheart Street, Toxteth Park, Liverpool
d: 26 Aug 1902 in 20 Lockheart Street, Toxteth Park, Liverpool

Joseph Lennon
b: Mar 1904 in 28 Denton Street, Toxteth Park, Liverpool
d: 10 Aug 1904 in 28 Denton Street, Toxteth Park, Liverpool

George Lennon
b: 14 Aug 1905 in 28 Denton Street, Toxteth Park, Liverpool
d: 1956 in Copperfield Street, Toxteth, Liverpool

Herbert Lennon
b: 18 Apr 1908 in Toxteth Park, Liverpool
d: 1968 in Aberconwy, Wales

Sydney Lennon
b: 26 Jul 1909 in 27 Copperfield Street, Toxteth Park, Liverpool
d: Oct 2003 in London, Ontario, Canada

Harold Lennon
b: Dec 1910 in 27 Copperfield Street, Toxteth Park, Liverpool
d: 21 Aug 1911 in 27 Copperfield Street, Toxteth Park, Liverpool

Alfred Lennon
b: 14 Dec 1912 in 27 Copperfield Street, Toxteth Park, Liverpool
d: 01 Apr 1976 in Brighton, Sussex

Edith Lennon
b: 21 Mar 1915 in 27 Copperfield Street, Toxteth Park, Liverpool
d: 1980 in Aberconwy, Wales

Charles Lennon
b: 25 Nov 1918 in 27 Copperfield Street, Toxteth Park, Liverpool
d: 26 May 2002 in Liverpool

The sixteen children of John Lennon's enigmatic grandfather Jack, nine of whom sadly died in infancy. The fate of eldest daughter Mary Elizabeth Lennon, the only surviving child of his first marriage, is not known, though she is believed to have immigrated. Eldest surviving son George Lennon, a Dock Labourer, died of tuberculosis, at the age of fifty, in the family home at 27 Copperfield Street. He was nursed in his final days by youngest brother Charlie Lennon, who became a much-loved local character in Liverpool, always happy to mingle and talk with Beatles fans.

Unlike John Lennon's father Alf, Edith Lennon used her Blue Coat School education to pursue a successful white-collar career, becoming a teacher in North Wales, brother Herbert also later joining her there in his retirement. Sydney Lennon, who had at one time hoped to adopt the young John Lennon, left Liverpool for Canada in 1967, at the height of the Beatles fame, and was the last of the Lennon siblings to die, aged ninety-three, in October 2003. Unlike younger brother Charlie, he preferred privacy and had shunned any Beatles related publicity, though was nevertheless proud of his world-famous nephew.

[35]

The Stanleys

Julia Stanley, John Lennon's mother, was born on the 12th March 1914, at number 8 Head Street, Toxteth, Liverpool, the sixth of seven children born to George Ernest Stanley, a Sailor in the Merchant Navy, and his wife Annie. By a strange quirk of fate, the mother of one Liverpool legend was born three years to the day, and just one street away, from another, rather more infamous character of local legend, William Patrick *'Paddy'* Hitler, the son of the great dictators' elder brother Alois Hitler who had moved to Liverpool at the beginning of the 20th century and married a local Irish girl.

Whether these two neighbouring children, with shared birthdays, one nephew to Europe's most wicked tyrant, the other mother to one of the centuries most loved musical icons, would ever have met or crossed paths in their formative years, can only be guessed at, though given John's own later interest in Hitler (born in a Nazi air raid, he delighted in doing a comic impersonation of him, and even tried without success to have his image added to the Sergeant Pepper Album cover) it is nevertheless one of the more bizarre coincidences in the wider Beatles story.

The Stanley family themselves were at one time one of the most ancient and influential families in all of Great Britain. Important land owners in Saxon England, they rose to hold prestigious titles such as the Lord Lieutenants of Ireland, the Earls of Derby, and the Kings of Mann, in the centuries immediately following the Norman conquest.

Sir Thomas Stanley, Earl of Derby, 1435-1504, his betrayal of King Richard III was instrumental in placing the Tudor dynasty on the throne of England

In the middle ages, they were instrumental in placing the Tudor dynasty on England's throne, playing a decisive role at the Battle of Bosworth Field in 1485, Sir Thomas Stanley plucking the crown of England from the slain body of Richard III, last of the Plantagenet Kings, hunchbacked demon of Shakespearean tradition, placing it firmly upon the head of the victorious Lancastrian claimant, twenty-eight-year-old Welshman Henry Tudor.

Though it is claimed all Stanley's ultimately stem from this same aristocratic route, certainly by the time John Lennon's mother's family first appear in the historical record, it is in far more humble circumstances. The first of John Lennon's Stanley ancestors whose details can be positively traced, his great-great grandfather, William Henry Stanley, was in fact not from the north of England, but the South, being born in the year 1814, in the parish of St George's, Southwark, on the south bank of London's River Thames.

It appears that his parents, William and Isabella Stanley, were married ten years before this in Stroud, Gloucestershire, in England's rural West Country, and it can probably be assumed that like many such couples they had moved soon after, with their children, to the burgeoning confines of the nation's capital in search of work. From the records of his children's baptism in London, William appears to have been initially successful in this, eking out a trade for himself there as a jobbing Stonemason, but if he and his family had harboured dreams, like so many others coming to London, of streets paved with gold and comfortable living, then they were soon to be sorely disappointed, the family address given on the baptism of at least one of their children as the local Workhouse, then, as ever, the absolute last resort of any working class family driven to the extremes of desperation in times of dire poverty.

Baptism of John Lennon's great-great grandfather William Henry Stanley, in Lambeth, Surrey, now South London, August 1814. *London Metropolitan Archives, Reference Number: p85/mry1/350*

Perhaps as a result of these tough conditions William Stanley, senior, died whilst still relatively young, in 1832, at age of forty-eight. With younger siblings, it would have now been imperative for his eldest son William Henry, to move out from his family home as soon as possible, and ease the financial burden on his widowed mother, Isabella, which may well have influenced his decision, less than a year later, at age nineteen, to marry the twenty-three-year-old Elizabeth Miller, a fellow South Londoner, and thereafter set up home with her. On their wedding record his occupation was not given, though on the baptism of the couple's first son Edward, born five years later, in June 1837, just a fortnight before the eighteen-year-old Victoria took to the throne to begin the longest reign in British history, he was recorded as a Carpenter, so clearly had chosen not to follow his late father into the Stonemason's trade, perhaps wisely given the poverty his father had clearly endured by that chosen route.

Life as a Carpenter, though a respectable and important occupation, would nevertheless have been scarcely better paid than that of a Stonemason, and it was perhaps this realisation, coupled with a craving for a greater degree of stability for his young family than he himself had enjoyed, that led him to soon abandon this trade too, and instead maneuver himself towards the greater respectability and status of white collar work, finding employment for himself as a Solicitor's Clerk.

In the course of his new employment, a move away from the country's capital was necessitated, first to Birmingham, where two more children, a daughter Eliza, and a second son named for the father, William Henry Stanley, junior, were born to the couple, and then on again to nearby Coventry, where they are recorded together on the census of 1851.

Soon after, William's wife, Elizabeth Stanley, died, and in the wake of this sad event the family moved again, for a final time, ten miles away to the small midlands village of Chilvers Coton, just outside the town of Nuneaton. The 1861 census records them there, William Henry Stanley now forty-six, a widow, with his two youngest children Eliza, fourteen, and William Henry, junior, thirteen. Missing from the family home was eldest son Edward, by this time twenty-three, and the same year's census reveals he, in a move as far removed from his father's life as possible, had taken to a life on the seas as a Mariner.

[37]

This eventually, perhaps inevitably, led him to the great dock city of Liverpool, and whilst there he was married in the September of 1866, aged twenty-nine, to twenty-two-year-old Mary Ann Lucy Gildea. Interestingly on the marriage record he gave his father's occupation not as a Solicitor's Clerk, but as an Actor, making William Henry Stanley, senior, John Lennon's great-great grandfather, the only one of any of the Beatles ancestors to be documented as ever being employed in any area of the creative arts.

Marriage of Edward Stanley and Mary Gildea, St Simon's, Liverpool 1866, Edward's father, John Lennon's great-great grandfather, William Henry Stanley recorded as an actor. *Liverpool Record Office ref 283 SIM/3/3*

Younger brother William Henry Stanley, junior, John Lennon's great-grandfather, was by this point nineteen, and may well have travelled to Liverpool from Chilvers Coton to witness his brother marry. It's likely he decided to stay on thereafter, and the reason for this was almost certainly Mary Ann's younger sister Eliza, also nineteen, love quickly blossoming between the pair, they too, like their elder siblings, being married in Liverpool, just over two years later.

The Gildea sisters, like their new husbands, were not natives of Liverpool, in their case coming from an Irish family, though unlike the Irish roots on John Lennon's father's side, his mother's Gildea family came from a very different cultural tradition and community there. Though the name itself is indicative of native Irish Catholic origin, coming from the Gaelic *Mac giolla Dhe*, *'Son of God's Servant'*, originally a sept of the O'Donnell's originating in Donegal, in the far North of the Isle, certainly by the time Eliza's father, Lennon's great-great grandfather, Charles Gildea, was born in the late 1790s, they had very much become part of the dominant Protestant Ascendancy in the Isles.

The plantation of Ireland, the organized colonization, particularly of the Ulster Province in the North of the country, by Protestant settlers from mainland Britain, first began in earnest under the Welsh Tudor Monarchy, and was heavily expanded and consolidated under the Scottish Stuart King James I (1603-1625). The bulk of Ireland's existing native population, still staunch in their adherence to both Pope and Roman Catholicism, were largely disinherited in the process, part of a brutal policy intended to both *'pacify'* and *'civilise'* the Irish, imposed upon them in the wake of the ill-fated rebellion by the U'Niell clan of the North against Tudor rule, undertaken in the closing decade of the 16th century, which had been supported by several hostile Catholic powers in mainland Europe. This process was to ultimately lay the root foundations of much of the sectarian division and troubles in Northern Ireland which remain largely unresolved to this day.

Though the repression of the native Gaelic language and culture in Ireland was often overt and brutal in nature, the British Crown also frequently employed much subtler methods to stamp out resistance to their

[38]

rule, employing a carrot and stick strategy toward the indigenous population. Whereas the practice of Catholicism itself was never outright banned, the Catholic Irish nevertheless were barred from voting, holding any public office or position, fined if caught practicing their faith and, in a measure many found particularly irksome, were made to pay enforced tithes for the upkeep of the Protestant Church in Ireland.

This situation was made worse still in 1703, when the Popery Act was passed. This prohibited the eldest son of a Catholic landowner from inheriting his father's estate whole unless he first converted to Protestantism. If he refused to do so the land would be subdivided equally amongst all surviving sons. The aim of this was twofold, to encourage new conversions to the Protestant faith, whilst at the same time weakening further the few remaining big landed Catholic estates, by then barely 15% of the land, subtly and gradually shrinking their size down to nothing, a highly effective, but ultimately disastrous, policy which can be argued laid the seeds of the catastrophic potato famine of the following century.

British Protestant planters massacred by native Irish Catholic uprising, Ulster, 1641

This plethora of hated discriminatory measures imposed upon the Irish, were dubbed *'The Penal Laws'*, and may explain why John Lennon's branch of the Gildea's had converted to Protestantism by the late 18th century, a fact evidenced by William Gildea, John's 3 x great-grandfather, appearing listed as both a Voter and Landowner in the rural parish of Roscor, County Fermanagh, in 1788, when he would have been just eighteen years of age. This would not have been possible were he a Catholic, and since the Gildea family were not listed amongst the Protestant English and Scot's settlers that were granted land parcels in this area during the 17th century colonisation of the land, it would appear that William and his family were one of the few remaining native Irish Catholic landowners in the area, and that at this time William, the eldest son, chose to convert in order to fully inherit his father's estate.

The degree to which William Gildea's conversion was one of necessity or choice can then only be guessed at, but certainly the family he raised soon embraced both their new community and status. Though William married twice, his first wife's name is not noted in the patchy church records which survive for the parish, though it is known they had at least two children together, a son Thomas, born in 1790, and another son Charles, John Lennon's great-great grandfather, born in the late summer of 1798.

Roscor, Magheracross, Fermanagh, Northern Ireland. Birth place of John Lennon's great-great grandfather Charles Gildea, summer 1798.
Photo Kenneth Allen

[39]

This was at the height of yet another momentous point in Ireland's ever turbulent history, the uprising of the United Ireland Movement, against British rule, led by a charismatic legal student of English and French Huguenot descent, Theobald Wolfe Tone, which began in April of that year, and by summer, with the assistance of an invasion force from revolutionary France, had turned into the most concentrated outbreak of violence in Irish history and the biggest threat to British and Protestant interests in the land for over a century. Though the rebel forces, allied with the French, won great victories at the Battle of Castlebar, on August 27th 1798, in County Mayo, and Battle of Collooney, a week later in County Sligo, the British soon turned the tables, inflicting almost total defeat on the rebels at the battle of Ballinamuck, in county Longford, just days later. Bloody reprisals and summary executions then swept the land, with the total death toll from the three-month rebellion estimated as high as fifty thousand.

1798 Uprising in Ireland, a landmark in Irish history, which led directly to the total loss of Irish independence three years later, the entire country swallowed up in the United Kingdom for more than a century afterwards.

It was into this mass turmoil Charles Gildea was born, though how it affected him and his family is unknown. Little in fact can be known for sure about his early years, aside from the fact his mother had sadly died by the time he was nine and a half years of age, his father William at this time being remarried, on 24th April 1808 in Magheracross' Church of Ireland Protestant church, the bride's name on this occasion noted in the records, as Ann Chitck. The couple had one further child together, a younger half-sister for Charles, Margaret Gildea, born later the same year.

Charles Gildea next appears in the records around his eighteenth birthday, in August 1816, at which time he made his way to Enniskillen Castle, a few miles from his home in Roscor, and volunteered for service in the British Army, being noted at the time as "*5 feet 7 and a half tall, brown eyes, fair complexion, by trade a Clerk*". Elder brother Thomas was already serving in the 8th foot regiment, having joined up six years earlier, clearly displaying how integrated the family had now become in the Protestant community.

Duly attested, Charles was billeted as a Private in the 6th Regiment Dragoons. Colloquially known as *The Enniskillen Dragoons,* this regiment were amongst the most famous in the British Army, and of particular importance to the Protestant Loyalist community of Ireland. Formed in the 1680s during the Williamite War, when the Dutch Protestant Prince William of Orange fought his dethroned Catholic uncle James II, for control of the British Crown, recruits swore a specific oath on *'The Holy Evangelists'* to "d*efend the Protestant Religion and interest in Ireland, to the utmost of their power and ability, with life and fortune, against all that should endeavour to subvert the same.'*

[40]

Enniskillen Castle, built in the 15th century, by the Irish Maguire family, whom, coincidentally, John Lennon also descends from. After the colonisation of Ulster it became a British Army Garrison. It flies the English flag of St George to this day.

Within weeks of their formation, the Enniskillen Dragoons were instrumental in relieving their fellow Protestants in Derry, who had been besieged by James' troops for one hundred and five days, and with a staunch refusal to capitulate to the enemy, had endured starvation and disease, ultimately suffering over three thousand deaths, a quarter of the entire city's population.

A year later in 1690 they again played a decisive role in Irish and European history at the Battle of Boyne, which saw the total defeat of King James, who fled into permanent exile to the court of his cousin Louis XIV of France, effectively ending the Catholic cause in Britain for good, and setting the Protestant community in a position of undisputed dominance in Ireland for the next two centuries.

Enniskillen Dragoons in action against the French, Battle of Warburg, Germany, 31st July 1760

A century later, in 1815, just a year before the young Charles Gildea joined their ranks, the Dragoons had once more distinguished themselves, this time fighting alongside English and Scottish Dragoon regiments, putting down the cavalry forces of Emperor Napoleon Bonaparte at the Battle of Waterloo.

Doubtless, well aware of the prestige and history of the regiment he was joining, Charles was a keen recruit and soon settled into his new role, spending just under eight years serving diligently with them. Eventually, at the age of twenty-five, he was promoted up the ranks, to the position of Sergeant, and at the same time transferred from the Dragoons to the 99th Regiment of Foot, newly formed that year in Glasgow, following a request from the Governor of Mauritius, a British colony, for urgent reinforcements. After two years of preparations, Charles and his regiment were posted to this small tropical island, a full five hundred miles off the coast of East Africa in the Indian Ocean, and here he would ultimately spend the next eleven years of his life.

First settled by Dutch colonists in the 17th century, Mauritius was claimed for the French East Indian Company in 1715, who set up mass sugar plantations and imported slaves there in great numbers from neighbouring Mozambique and Madagascar. It soon became a profitable colony for the French Government, who took over official control from the company in 1767, and during the Napoleonic wars, an important naval base for them too. This led to its capture by the British, in 1810, and its eventual incorporation into the British Empire, under the Treaty of Paris, in 1814. Nevertheless, French institutions, including the Napoleonic Code of Law, were maintained and the French language remained the common day to day *lingua de franca* of most the populace.

Port Louis, Mauritius, 1831, at the time Charles Gildea was stationed there.

Engraved by William Rider

Depiction of Slavery in Mauritius 1818.

Engraving from Louis de Freycinet, Voyage Autour du Monde, Atlas Historique

Contemporary depiction of the evils of the African slave trade.

Originally published in London, April 10th 1792

The ABOLITION of the SLAVE TRADE.

[43]

Though the British officially abolished the slave trade on taking over in 1810, and fresh imports of slaves ceased, as in other British colonies the domestic institution of slavery itself continued, and by the time Charles Gildea arrived there approximately 85% of the population were African slaves, some seventy-eight thousand persons, a highly intense concentration for a small island of just seven hundred and twenty square miles. The local slave market, where males were sold separately, women and children together, saw nearly three thousand individuals bought and sold in the years between 1825 and 1835.

In spite of the profitability to them of the sugar trade, the British government, now firmly opposed to slavery, wanted the institution abolished altogether, and accordingly ordered it to be put to an outright end in all their colonies in 1832. On Mauritius, like elsewhere in the empire, this edict faced considerable local opposition from the powerful vested interests and was not easily enforced. It was in this extremely turbulent transitional period in the island's history, overseeing the abolition of slavery, that Sergeant Charles Gildea primarily found himself involved.

No exact detail of his time there is known, but it cannot have been uneventful. He was stripped of his stripes and rank in the spring of 1833, at the same time the order to end the slave trade first began to be enforced on the island, and demoted back down to Private, the lowest rank in the service. Though he swiftly re-earned his stripes, being promoted to Corporal after another nine months, and again to his former rank Sergeant after eighteen months, this must surely have been a humiliating process none the less, and it is puzzling as to what provoked this, his records unfortunately offering no further clue.

Despite the heavy opposition, after three years the slave trade of Mauritius had been effectively stamped out, with cheap labour from another British colony, India, bought in to replace the lost slave labour, and the masters, though not the slaves themselves, paid what was deemed suitable reparation for lost earnings. The situation on the island had quieted considerably by 1837, and as a result Charles Gildea and his regiment were finally stood down, making the return voyage, home to Ireland, in July of that year.

Once back home it was clear that Charles, though still only thirty-nine years of age, had been severely affected by this time in foreign service, and he spent much of the next year in the army sick bay. In May of the following year he applied to leave the service on grounds of his ill health, his commanding officer sending the following graphic description of his plight to their superiors in Dublin at that time:

Sergeant Charles Gildea, aged 39. - He has been twenty-one years and nine months in actual service, or twenty-seven years and six months allowing two years to reckon for three in a tropical climate eastward of the Cape. During the period he was at Mauritius, he had several attacks of dysentery, and a liver complaint. Since he returned home he has had a most severe pulmonic complaint which is in a great measure relieved, but lately his constitution is entirely undermined, face bloated swelling of the limbs, and abdomen, general debility, accompanied with visceral obstruction. He can scarcely walk, total loss of appetite, and his constitution is entirely worn out in the service. From the above statement it is evident he is totally unfit to perform the duty of a soldier. His complaint is not caused by vice or distemperance. - Head Quarters 12th May 1838, William Williams, Major of 99th Foot Regiment.

In the wake of his appeal, Charles was sent for in Dublin, where he was further examined by another medical board on 22nd June 1838, which confirmed he was suffering both pulmonic and visceral disease, and duly discharged him from service, with full pension, adding the following comments to his file:

According to the surgeon's report annexed it seems that this case of disease and disability was contracted in and by the service without being attributable to design, vice, neglect or distemperance or constitutional disease [...] Board is of the opinion that his conduct and character has been those of a good and efficient soldier, sober, trustworthy and seldom in hospital until of late years.

[44]

Original letter sent by Charles Gildea's commanding officer to Army H.Q Dublin May 1838, requesting his immediate discharge. *National Archives, Kew*

Having been in service for all his adult life, and now approaching his fortieth birthday in poor health, starting a family may have been the last thing on his mind, but this is exactly what Charles soon did, falling in love with and marrying, after a short courtship, Ann Rogers, the nineteen-year-old daughter of book keeper Robert Rogers, who like the Gildea's were part of Northern Ireland's Protestant community.

Their first son Charles Gildea, junior, was born in Londonderry, that same year, on 11th December 1839. Shortly after they moved to Anne's hometown, Omagh, County Tyrone, Charles finding work for himself there, in the Military Barracks at Drumragh, as a Clerk and Staff Sergeant Major for the Omagh district of the Chelsea Pensioners, the organisation which distributed pensions to elderly and infirm ex-soldiers such as him

[45]

In Omagh, Charles and Ann settled into married life, adding a further seven children to the family, six daughters and one more son. Eliza Gildea, John Lennon's great-grandmother, christened as Elizabeth Jane Gildea, was their third child, born to the couple in the year 1846. At around the time their youngest daughter Juliana was born, in 1858, eldest son, Charles, junior, left the family home, and became the first Gildea to cross the water to Liverpool, initially finding work for himself in the city as an assistant to a Provision Dealer, and marrying there, two years later to a local Blacksmith's daughter Margaret Blackburn. By that time in Ireland his father Charles' health had begun to decline dramatically.

St. Columba's Church, Drumragh, Omagh, Co Tyrone, John Lennon's great-grandmother, Elizabeth Jane Gildea, was baptised here on the 26th March 1846. *Photo John Campbell*

[46]

In view of the various ailments he had picked up as a result of his army service, Charles, senior, had in many ways done well to raise a large family and survive for as long as he had. In 1855 his father William had died, aged eighty-four, followed by his sister Margaret, twelve months later, at forty-eight, and his step mother Ann too not long afterwards. Whether this hastened his own decline is not known, but he was not long in following, passing away on 8th March 1861 at the age of sixty-two, leaving instructions to be buried in the same shared grave as his father, sister and stepmother, in the local churchyard of his birth, Magheracross, County Fermanagh.

Magheracross Graveyard, County Fermanagh, Ireland, last resting place of John Lennon's great-great grandfather Charles Gildea, and great-great-great grandfather William Gildea.

Though he had left what small provision he could for his widow Ann in his will, this was obviously never going to be sufficient for her to raise their seven children on her own, the eldest of which was still only seventeen, the youngest just two, so Ann made the fateful decision to move with her family, to Liverpool, where her eldest son Charles, could both assist and provide for them.

Charles now in business for himself as a Game and Poultry Merchant, the same year appears in the *Liverpool Mercury* of 8th November 1861, which records him being fined five pounds for illegally altering his scales in his favour at St John's Market by pasting a penny to the bottom.

Once in Livepool, Ann settled in the streets surrounding the parish church of St Thomas, Toxteth, and was eventually remarried to local Church Clerk, Richard Maddocks, settling into a home together in middle class Kent Square, a small row of relatively fashionable Georgian houses.

She must have been pleased to see all her daughters marry and raise families and both her sons prosper there, Charles in his poultry business, despite his somewhat creative approach to business practice, youngest son Isaac taking to the seas in the Merchant Service, eventually migrating as a young man to Canada with his wife, and later settling in to a comfortable family life in Washington, USA.

Despite this, the Gildea family clearly did not forget Ireland, or indeed let go of some of the more ingrained beliefs and attitudes they had acquired there. Charles Gildea, junior, was an active member of the Liverpool branch of the Orange Order, an organisation dedicating to preserving the Protestant Supremacy in Ireland, even signing the Ulster Covenant of 1912 from his home in Liverpool, pledging his opposition to the '*threat*' of Irish home rule by the Catholic majority, and his willingness to defend Ulster in this eventuality.

[47]

Covenant :—

BEING CONVINCED in our consciences that Home Rule would be disastrous to the material well-being of Ulster as well as of the whole of Ireland, subversive of our civil and religious freedom, destructive of our citizenship, and perilous to the unity of the Empire, we, whose names are underwritten, men of Ulster, loyal subjects of His Gracious Majesty King George V., humbly relying on the God whom our fathers in days of stress and trial confidently trusted, do hereby pledge ourselves in solemn Covenant, throughout this our time of threatened calamity, to stand by one another in defending, for ourselves and our children, our cherished position of equal citizenship in the United Kingdom, and in using all means which may be found necessary to defeat the present conspiracy to set up a Home Rule Parliament in Ireland. And in the event of such a Parliament being forced upon us, we further solemnly and mutually pledge ourselves to refuse to recognise its authority. In sure confidence that God will defend the right, we hereto subscribe our names.

And further, we individually declare that we have not already signed this Covenant.

The Ulster Covenant of September 1912, signed by nearly half a million Ulster Protestants, was a response to the Home Rule Bill, and the beginning of Ireland's slide into Civil War, sowing the seeds of the eventual partition of the land. John Lennon's great uncle, Charles Gildea, was one of the few outside Ireland to sign, as one of the 286 Ulster Protestant Liverpudlians in the Liverpool branch of the Pro-British Orange Order.

PRONI

Mary and Eliza Gildea, Ann's two eldest daughters, after their respective marriages to the two Stanley brothers, settled down in to their new homes a few streets away from each other in Liverpool's Everton district. Whilst Edward Stanley at first continued to serve at sea, William Stanley tried to find work for himself following in their father's footsteps as a Solicitor's Clerk, the 1871 census recording him thus, though adding in brackets 'unemployed', so clearly, he was finding this difficult.

Perhaps due to this, before long both brothers were instead being recorded as Freight Clerks at the Liverpool docks, the same occupation followed by John Lennon's paternal grandfather Jack Lennon. Though certainly a step up from the Dock Labourers, the Freight Clerks were nevertheless not on the same level of white collar respectability or pay as Solicitor's Clerks.

In 1876, after just ten years of marriage, Mary Gildea Stanley sadly died. To help cope with his loss, Edward Stanley moved into his brother William's home at Abbey Street, Everton, with his two young sons Edward, seven, and Clarence, four, the family's grief compounded there further still, the following year, by the death of young Clarence.

By this point, William and Eliza Stanley had three children themselves, all sons, the youngest George Ernest Stanley, John Lennon's grandfather, then two years old. Another five children would later be born to them there, including twins, though their family too would face tragedy, only two of these children surviving into adulthood, alongside their elder siblings, a son Albert, and a daughter Charlotte.

[48]

Contemporary depiction of a Freight Clerk at work on the Liverpool Docks, circa 1880.

William Stanley had evidently found regular employment as a Freight Clerk just as difficult to secure as that of a Solicitor's Clerk, and after brief stints labouring in the dock warehouses, he eventually followed in his elder brother's early footsteps, finding work as a Sailor on the freight and cargo ships and leaving his family for the sea shortly before his fortieth birthday.

This seems to have marked a watershed point in his and Eliza's marriage, and by 1891 she had moved with the children, away from the family home in Everton, to Upper Frederick Street in Toxteth, just a street away from Kent Square where her mother Ann and her younger unmarried Gildea sisters lived. Though she still described herself as married on that year's census, and this move may have simply been intended to be nearer to her own family for support during her husband's absence at sea, by 1901 this was clearly not the case.

On that year's census, now describing herself as widowed, she was using the surname of another man, Abramson, a Swedish Mariner. She would again use his surname when she witnessed her youngest daughter Charlotte's wedding in 1910, though she later reverted to her married name Stanley on the 1911 census, and it was also used on her death certificate of 1916.

What exactly had happened to husband William in the intervening years? Her claim to be widowed, at least, does not seem to hold true. The1901 Census finds him back on shore, and boarding at the *Prince of Wales Beer and Lodging House*, Peterborough, earning his living there working as a Musician, the only Beatle ancestor ever officially recorded doing so. Five years later son George's wedding certificate also describes him as a Musician, though by the 1910 wedding of his daughter Charlotte Stanley, his trade was given as a Commercial Traveller.

The census of the following year, 1911 finds only one William Henry Stanley following this profession anywhere in England, though living not in Liverpool, but in London. Now in his sixties, he appears to have set up home there permanently with a lady near to thirty years his junior, Kathleen. Though they never married, the couple had at least two children together, Beatrice, born in 1899, and William, born in 1902.

[49]

It cannot be said with certainty that this is the same man, but it appears quite likely. Whether perhaps he met the younger Kathleen while docked in London, and abandoned wife Eliza in Liverpool for this new relationship, or just as possible his lengthy absences at sea had already put an untenable strain on their marriage long before this point, clearly by 1901 the evidence points towards William and Eliza Stanley having separated for good.

There is no evidence of the couple ever having officially divorced, then an expensive and difficult process for the working classes, and this perhaps explains why neither were able to give the stamp of legality to their respective later relationships, and why Eliza, at least, preferred to describe herself on official forms as widowed.

It may well have been at the same time of this parting, and Eliza's move to Toxteth to be near her mother, that the couple's son, George Stanley, then twelve, first met his future wife, thirteen-year-old Annie Millward, who lived, with her family, at 17 Kent Square, just a few doors along from the Gildea's family home at no. 12.

Georgian housing in Kent Square, Toxteth, in the 1880s home to both the Millward and Gildea families, and a street away from the Stanley household, at Upper Frederick Street. Photograph taken by Father d'Andria, parish priest of St Peter's Church, Liverpool in 1930.

Liverpool Record Office

Annie Jane Millward, maternal grandmother of John Lennon, was never truly to know the future Beatle, as sadly she died of a brain hemorrhage when he was just six months old. She was the first child to her parents, John and Mary Millward, the family moving together, whilst she was still a baby, to Liverpool. She was born, in the June of 1873, in Cheshire, at the *Bear and Billet Inn and Public House*. This historic timber-framed building was built in 1664 as the town residence of the Earls of Shrewsbury, and was later converted to an inn and public house in the early 18th century.

It has been claimed Annie was born here because her father, John Millward, was employed in service to the Earls of Shrewsbury, but this is more than likely myth, as the Earls had severed their last link to the building a full six years before Annie's birth. John and his wife appear to have been simply lodging there at the time, John describing himself as a '*Gentleman*' on her birth certificate, someone not in active employment, but instead living off an independent source of wealth.

Bear and Billet Inn, Chester, Cheshire,
birthplace in 1873 of John Lennon's
grandmother Annie Jane Millward

Despite these links to both Chester and Liverpool, the censuses reveal both Annie's parents were originally natives of Wales. Previous researchers have struggled to positively identify them, due to the fact they did not ever marry, and without a marriage certificate, one of the fundamental building blocks of genealogy, there has been a certain amount of guess work as to their parentage.

Existing accounts of Lennon's ancestry have sometimes identified Annie's father as John Dembry Millward, the son of Evan Millward, a Glamorgan publican and his wife Mary Dembry. The pub Evan Millward ran in South Wales celebrates the link, and a recent television program in Wales stated this as fact. Unfortunately it is not the case, this man certainly did exist but was provably elsewhere when John Lennon's namesake great-grandfather was living in Liverpool, and in fact never strayed very far from his home in South Wales, dying a few miles from his birth place, a forty six-year-old unmarried bachelor, at his sister's household in 1883.

Despite the lack of a marriage certificate a closer look at the census records do reveal both Annie Millward's parents, in fact, gave their place of origin as North Wales, John Millward as Rhyl, Flintshire, on the 1891 census, and Mary Millward as Betws, Denbighshire, on the 1911 census.Accordingly both are found in these places on the census which was taken closest to Annie's birth, 1871, John Millward being counted that year at 30 Water Street, Rhyl, Flintshire and Mary, a mere ten miles away, at her family home, the farmstead of Ty Celyn (in English 'Holly House'), in Betws yn Rhos, Denbighshire.

John Lennon's great-grandfather John Millward, on the 1871 Census, 30 Water Street, Rhyl, Wales.
Crown Copyright, Class: RG10; Piece: 5668; Folio: 108; Page: 39; GSU roll: 892492

[51]

The reasons behind the couple never having married, and John's status as 'Gentleman' at the time of Annie's birth, also perhaps become a little clearer through a closer inspection of these same records. John Millward, who at thirty-six, was sixteen years older than Mary, was recorded as a widow that year, living on the 'interest of money'. It has not proved possible to identify his first marriage, but his sixty six-year-old sister-in-law is recorded in the household, so it may be his first wife was considerably older and he had inherited his wealth, perhaps including this seaside property in Rhyl, from her.

This census shows John himself originally came from St Asaph, just a few miles south of Rhyl. The parish records there reveal his branch of the Millward family had been living in St Asaph at least since the mid-18th century, as tenants on the farmstead of Faenol Fawr, Glascoed, where they were in service as Farmers and Gardeners on the Bodelwyddan estate of the Welsh William's family.

The originator of that line, Sir William Williams, rose from humble Town Solicitor to become the Speaker of the Commons under King Charles II, Solicitor General to James II, and finally Lord Lieutenant of Merionethshire. He built the family's main residence as St Asaph, Bodelwyddan House, around the year 1690. The house later underwent major renovation, giving it the current appearance of a 'mock' medieval castle, under the incumbent at the time of John Millward's birth, Sir John Hay Williams (1794-1859), who was of a similarly high social standing, serving variously as High Sheriff of Anglesey (1832), Flintshire (1836), and Denbighshire (1839).

Employed by the Williams', John Millward's father, Thomas, a Professional Gardener, had originally been in charge of the gardens at Bodelwyddan House, but in 1830 when Sir John inherited the estate from his father and began his ambitious renovation, he instead placed him at nearby Bontnewydd, to cultivate the flower gardens at another of the Williams' estates, Dolben Hall, inherited from Emma Dolben, mother of Sir William Williams. It was within this impressive ten-bedroom mansion, set on the picturesque banks of the River Elwy, that John Lennon's great-grandfather first entered the world around the year 1834. This same small area has since become of international importance, the caves situated on the grounds, when excavated in 1978, being found to contain the most westerly remains of early man discovered anywhere in Europe, dating to near a quarter of a million years in age.

Faenol Fawr Country House, Glascoed, Bodelwyddan, North Wales, painted in 1776, and pictured today. John Lennon's Millward family had their home on the estate here from at least the 1740s.

Bodelwyddan Castle, built in the late 17th century, home of the Aristocratic Williams family in North Wales.

Photo Dot Potter

The sculptured gardens at Bodelwyddan Castle, St Asaph, North Wales. These were in the charge of John Lennon's great-great-grandfather, Thomas Millward, in the early decades of the 19th century.

Photo Dot Potter

[53]

Sir John Hay Williams (1794-1859). His diaries record a lifelong obsession with beautifying the grounds and gardens of his estate at Bodelwyddan, on which he spent enormous amounts of time and money. Erecting an ingenious limestone wall, he effectively created a central heated garden, a full half century before his house enjoyed the same luxury. This allowed him to grow early blossom peaches, apricots and nectarines, as well as an extensive selection of rare plants, fauna & orchids. Invaluable in assisting him in this was his head gardener, Thomas Millward, great-great grandfather of John Lennon. In his dairy of 1844, Sir John speaks with great regret at having to retire to pension *'Old Thomas of the Gardens'* who had been recently taken ill. *Bodelwyddan Castle Trust*

By the time of the 1851 census Thomas Millward, John Lennon's great-great grandfather, who had married relatively late in life, was sixty-three, and retired on a lifelong pension by the grateful Williams family, living in a more modest home in nearby Roe, St Asaph. John Millward was counted there that year with his parents, aged sixteen, following the occupation of an Attorney's Clerk, the same profession later recorded for him in Liverpool.

Quite possibly it was the patronage of the William's family, with their legal background and connections, which provided him the necessary means and education to enter into this white-collar career, where his duties would have mostly consisted of taking shorthand notes for the legal representatives employing him during client's court proceedings.

That he was able to follow the above profession at all, in later life, seems extraordinary in light of another factor, which the 1871 census does not reveal, but a local newspaper report of the time sheds some light upon. Just two months before the census was taken, whilst out in the local countryside on a rook shooting expedition with some friends, travelling on horse and cart, John had suffered a dire mishap when the locking mechanism on his gun failed, and as a result the weapon had fully discharged itself, at close range, into his body. The wound had been so severe his life was for some time in danger, and in order to save him, the attending surgeons had been forced to amputate his entire left arm.

Water Street, Rhyl, turn of the 20th century. A popular seaside resort in North Wales, John Lennon's great-grandfather was recorded here on the census of 1871, recuperating from his recent shooting accident.

When and where he met Annie Millward's mother Mary is unknown, his parents' home at St Asaph was just a few miles east of hers at Betws yn Rhos, though perhaps she too had travelled the short distance up the coast to Rhyl, like many unmarried women of her age looking for work in service, and having helped nurse him back to health, a relationship had then developed between them, followed shortly by both pregnancy and elopement. This situation, minus elopement, mirrors almost exactly that of John Lennon's paternal grandparents, Jack and Polly Lennon, and was far from uncommon, though would have still, inevitably, been viewed unfavourably amongst their neighbours, family and peers, Victorian morality, and its manifest hypocrisies, at its height at this time.

Whatever the exact detail of their meeting and the domestic arrangements leading up to their first daughter Annie's birth, one thing is certain, this would not have been the first time John Lennon's great-grandmother, Mary, had, in her young life, been touched by scandal.

Born Mary Elizabeth Morris, in April 1851, she was the only surviving daughter of Welsh farmer William Morris, and his wife Ann Roberts. Her baptism at Llysfaen Parish Church records her abode as Lletty Du, a fifty-seven-acre farm, in Llanelian yn Rhos, Denbighshire, owned by her grandfather Richard Morris.

1851 april 13. No. 696.	Mary Elizabeth daut. of	William & Ann	Morris	Letty du	Farmer	E. Oldfield Rec.t

Baptism of John Lennon's great-grandmother Mary Elizabeth Morris, April 1851, Llysfaen Parish Church, Denbighshire, North Wales. *Denbighshire Records Office*

Originally a farm labourer, Richard Morris had married into a wealthy local family in the winter of 1821, his bride, Elizabeth Bridge, being the daughter of a prosperous Gentleman Farmer and County Auctioneer, Lynch Bridge. At the time of his own marriage, as a young man in the 1790s, Lynch, Lennon's 4 x great-grandfather was briefly working as a Mariner, and though he returned to Wales soon after, his marriage nevertheless took place in Liverpool, at St Peter's, giving John Lennon his oldest known ancestral link to the city of his birth.

The same forebear Lynch Bridge, also provides Lennon with his most illustrious set of ancestors. Baptised in Llanrwst, North Wales, by his maternal grandfather in 1765, the Reverend Richard Farrington, Lynch has an entry in the 1914 work *Pedigrees of Anglesey and Carnarvonshire Families* by John Edwards Griffith, F.L.S, which claims to be '*compiled from authentic and reliable sources*'. This work traces his ancestry through his great-grandmother, Elizabeth Jones of Anglesey, the Reverend Richard Farrington's mother, to most of the royal families of Pre-Conquest Wales.

If this account of Lynch's heritage is to be believed, this would make John Lennon both a direct descendant of Tudur *ap* Gruffudd "*Fychan*", Lord of Gwyddelwern, killed at the Battle of Battle of Pwll Melyn in 1405, brother of Wales's national hero, Owain Glyndŵr, and through him, Rhys *ap* Tewdwr, the 11th century Welsh Prince who was ancestor to the Tudor dynasty of England. This latter link, by extension, also makes Lennon a distant relation to the current ruling royal family of Great Britain.

Owain Glyndwr (1349-1416), Rebel Prince, Welsh National Hero, Great Uncle of John Lennon?
Photo Jeremy Bullwell

Whether true or not, and it is of course wise to retain a healthy dose of skepticism towards the accuracy of Victorian and Edwardian Royal pedigrees, certainly Lennon's 6 x great-grandfather Richard Farrington is in himself an extremely interesting individual. He was born in 1702 in Bridge Street, Chester, curiously the very same street where the *Bear and Billet Inn* stands and his descendant Annie Millward, Lennon's grandmother, would be born 170 years later. Since his father Robert was a Vintner and the *Bear and Billet* was by then an alehouse it is quite possible he was born in the very same place.

As a young man Richard was sent to be educated at Jesus College, Oxford University, and on completion of his studies, in 1724, he was ordained as an Anglican Minister. He held several posts in England, before at the age of forty-six returning to North Wales, his mother's homeland, becoming the Minister of Llanwnda in Cearnarvon. There he lived in a grand and beautiful country estate at Dinas Dinoethwy, which later became the residence of the Earls of Snowden, and was the childhood home of Princess Margaret's husband Lord Snowden. This would be the first, but favourite, of several parishes under his care in North Wales, before in his sixties he was promoted to the prestigious position of Chancellor of Bangor Cathedral. Aged seventy he returned to England, retiring to Bath, perhaps for the famous restorative health qualities that town boasted, and there ended his days, though he was body was transported back to Wales for burial alongside his first wife at Llanwnda Churchyard.

The Reverend Richard Farrington (1702-1772)

Engraving Courtesy of National Library of Wales

Alongside his religious duties, Reverend Farrington was also a noted Author. Before the move to Wales he had published a popular collection of twenty sermons in London, and once in Caernarvonshire, he had become fascinated by its history and particularly the area's links to the early Celtic Druids, seeking out relics and sites connected to them whenever and wherever he could. Several of his original works on this subject are much admired and are now housed in the National Library of Wales, including *Numismata Dinlleana*, *The Druid Monuments of Snowdonia* and *Celtic Antiquities of Snowdonia*. Through his second marriage, he had also become something of a businessman, purchasing several copper mines in the area, and it is probably through that route his daughter Mary met her husband William Bridge, who also owned and operated copper mines in the same region.

[57]

Plas Dinas, Dinas Dinoethwy, Llandwanda, Cearnarvonshire, North Wales. Home to John Lennon's 6 x great-grandfather, the Reverend Richard Farrington, and later, in the 20th century, the Earls of Snowdon.

Photo Andy Banner-Price

Despite this close link to the Anglican creed, Mary and William's son, the Reverend Farrington's grandson, Lynch Bridge, and his family, were later like many 19th century Welsh families, to adopt the non-conformist creed of Calvinistic Methodism, which spread like wild fire in Wales, with at least one of his sons becoming an active Methodist preacher in nearby Conway in the 19th century.

Lynch's daughter Elizabeth Bridge and new husband Richard Morris, John Lennon's 3 x great-grandparents, initially lived on the Bridge family farmstead at Ty'n Twll, Llanrwst after their marriage, before another local holding, six miles away, Lletty Du became available in 1827, and with help from his father-in-law, Richard was able to set himself up as a Gentleman Farmer there in his own right the following year. There Richard and Elizabeth raised seven children, including William Morris, John Lennon's great-great grandfather, who was just two years of age at the time of the move to Lletty Du, and who at the age of twenty-one, married Ann Roberts, the nineteen-year-old daughter of another local farmer, Richard Roberts of Llandrillo yn Rhos, who then held the smaller but picturesque farm, Berth y Glyd, in the nearby village of Llysfaen.

St Trillo's Chapel, Llandrillo yn Rhos, Denbighshire, in the village that was home to John Lennon's Welsh Roberts ancestors. One of the earliest Christian chapels in the British Isles, dating from the sixth century AD, this intriguing site is also the smallest Welsh chapel still in use, seating a maximum congregation of six.

Photo Jeff Buck

Tan Yr Allt Isa farm, Llandrillo yn Rhos, original home of the Roberts Family. John Lennon's 3 x great-grandfather, Richard Roberts, was born here in 1799, and his great-great grandmother, Ann Roberts, in 1827.

Aerial photo of Berth y Glyd Farm, Llysfaen, where Richard Roberts moved his family in the late 1830s. Here in 1851 Richard's daughter Ann, gave birth to John Lennon's great-grandmother Mary Elizabeth Morris, later the wife of John Millward. Demolished in the 1930s the site is now a council housing estate.

1851 Census: John Lennon's great-great grandparents, William and Ann Morris, at the farm of her parents Richard and Mary Roberts, Berth y Glyd, Llysfaen, Wales. Lennon's great-grandmother Mary was born to the couple just days later. *Crown Copyright HO107, Piece Number 2519, Folio 268, Page 34*

[59]

By the time John Lennon's great-grandmother Mary Elizabeth Morris was born in 1851, William and Ann Morris already had two elder children, both sons, Richard and John. At that point William still laboured at his father's farm, Lletty Du, and sometimes for his father-in-law at Berth y Glyd, but when Mary was still under a year old, like his father before him, William Morris was able to seize the opportunity to set himself up as a Gentleman Farmer in his own right, by purchasing the deeds to another local farmstead which had suddenly become available, Ty Celyn, in Betws yn Rhos, at nearly sixty acres equal to the size of his parent's farm and double that of his wife's families land at Berth y Glyd.

Sadly, Mary Elizabeth's early life there, on the surface, appears to have been relatively unhappy and plagued with ill fortune. A younger brother, Thomas Bridge Morris, was born within the first year, followed by two younger siblings, Ellen and William, who would both die in infancy. Not long after this, Mary's eldest brother Richard, aged ten, also died, followed by her mother two years later, at just thirty-three years of age. Mary was only nine years old herself at the time of her mother's loss and was left alone to look after her father, and her two surviving siblings, brothers John, eleven and Thomas, eight.

The family next appear in the records, a decade later, at the time of the 1871 census, still listed at Ty Celyn. As well as Mary Elizabeth, her brother, and her father, also recorded in the household was one-week old William Pierce Morris. The baptism records of the local church reveal he was an illegitimate child born to Mary, just a few days before her twentieth birthday. The father of the child was almost certainly William Pierce, the thirty-two-year-old unmarried son of Robert Pierce, a neighbouring farmer, who owned the much larger one hundred and forty-acre Peniarth Fawr, almost directly opposite to Ty Celyn.

Appearing neither on the birth certificate or baptism of Mary's child, William clearly refused to acknowledge his offspring, and the situation appears to have escalated further, three months after the birth, in July 1871, with the young Mary and William's mother, Ann Pierce, sixty-three, appearing in the local Magistrate's Court, each having summoned the other for an alleged assault. The bench rejected both claims, deciding each woman was as guilty as the other, and ordered them to cover their own costs, but the case was of sufficient local interest to be reported in the *North Wales Chronicle*.

ABERGELE.

Petty Sessions, Saturday, the 1st inst.—Before J. W. Wynne, B. W. Wynne, R. B. Hesketh, Esq., and the Rev. Thomas Williams.

Assault.—There were cross summonses in this case. Ann Pierce, Peniarthfawr, Bettws, charged Mary Morris, Tycolyn. The bench decided upon dismissing both cases, considering both in fault, and ordering each to pay their own costs.

North Wales Chronicle 8th July 1871, John Lennon's great-grandmother, Mary Elizabeth Morris, both accused and accuser, in a case of assault involving her neighbour, and likely grandmother of her illegitimate child, Ann Pierce. *British Newspaper Archive*

The scandal this would have been viewed with by her family, strict church going Methodists, can only be imagined, and clearly, she either chose to, or perhaps more likely, was forced to give this child up for adoption soon after. The situation is a sad mirror of that later faced by her own granddaughter, John Lennon's mother, Julia Lennon, who would find herself, nearly a century later, with a child born outside of marriage, Victoria, and likewise bowed to family pressure to have her adopted.

This first-born son of John Lennon's great-grandmother, William Pierce Morris, never married, and appears on all subsequent censuses as the adoptive son of John Jones, a Farm Labourer in nearby Abergele, and his wife Elizabeth. He remained in Abergele all his life, working as an Insurance Agent, and died shortly before his sixty eighth birthday, his will bequeathing all his possessions to the local Methodist Church. It seems likely he never regained contact with his birth mother or his half-siblings in Liverpool, including Lennon's grandmother Annie. It is doubtful he ever knew of their existence at all.

Perhaps this scandal is what encouraged Mary to leave her home and travel to Rhyl very soon after, ending up in the household of John Millward. Having struck up a relationship with the injured widower, sixteen years her senior, and again falling pregnant unmarried, keen to avoid further disgrace, the couple eloped, choosing to flee the local gossip mongers, and escape the disapproving stares and whispered comments altogether, by starting a new life together across the border, in England, first in Chester, perhaps for as long as John's private income allowed them to enjoy the comfortable lodgings at the prestigious *Bear and Billet*, and later, when funds ran dry, in more modest lodgings in Liverpool.

It may have been only a couple of hours away by road, but a large city like Liverpool was infinitely more accommodating to the victims of small time village scandals, here the past could be easily forgotten and buried, and the exact details of family arrangements might soon blend into a mere footnote, insignificant to the wider cacophony of urban life.

The 1881 census finds Mary and John Millward living together at 17 Kent Square, Toxteth, Liverpool, John once more working for his living, returning to his original profession as a Clerk in a Law Stationer's Office. As well as John Lennon's grandmother Annie, two more daughters, Mary Elizabeth Millward, and Harriet Catherine Ellenor Millward, had by that time been born to the family. A further two children George Gordon Millward, born winter that year, and John Bridge Millward, born in 1884, would later join them, though sadly John, the youngest, would die at just over a year of age.

1881 Census: John Millward, Mary Elizabeth Morris/Millward, and their three daughters, John Lennon's grandmother Annie Jane the eldest then aged 8, at their home 17 Kent Square, Toxteth, Liverpool
Crown Copyright, Class: RG11; Piece: 3616; Folio: 66; Page: 40; GSU roll: 1341866

Meanwhile, back in Wales, Mary's father William Morris had recently passed away, his death and that of his granddaughter being reported in local Welsh language newspapers in mid-March 1879:

March 9th, aged 53, Mr. William Morris, of Ty Celyn, Bettws, Abergele. Multiple tributes at his burial, gave testament to the character of this responsible and respected man in the eyes of his community, also on March 9th, aged thirteen months, Anne youngest child of Thomas Bridge Morris, of Ty Celyn, Abergele. She died, as can be seen, the same day as her grandfather, he died seven in the morning and she was flying to join him in 'a better world to live' the same evening.

According to the memoirs of John Lennon's sister, Julia Baird, Mary at some point received a generous financial bequest from an elder relative which allowed her to invest in several properties in Liverpool, renting them out as an independent and lucrative source of income. If this is true, her father was certainly not the source. His will left her just one guinea, roughly equivalent to just sixty UK Pounds or a hundred US Dollars at the time of writing, whilst the farm and the bulk of his estate instead went to her only surviving brother, Thomas Bridge Morris. This token amount perhaps suggests he had yet to forgive her for what he no doubt viewed as the shameful circumstances of her departure from their family home, and may have been a calculated move to prevent her making further claims on his estate, as she could have, legally, had he opted to omit her entirely.

Sadly, her brother Thomas soon followed their father and his infant daughter, three years later in 1882. At just thirty years of age his premature end was unexpected, and leaving no will, his estate and the Morris family farm at Ty Celyn passed in full to his pregnant widow, Elizabeth Morris Hughes, his first cousin, who already with a two-year-old son to support, seems fairly unlikely to have passed on any of her husband's estate to the out of favour Mary and her fledging family in Liverpool.

Another possible source may have been Mary's great uncle, William Bridge, the younger brother to her late grandmother Elizabeth, and indeed Julia Baird's account does cite a *'distant uncle'* as the mysterious benefactor. This gentleman, a retired Grocer and Book Seller, was the same son of Lynch Bridge, Gentleman Farmer, who had moved to Conway half a century earlier, to fulfill a ministry as a Methodist Preacher. He died in Liverpool in 1886, having joined his youngest daughter Ellen there, and left a healthy estate of nearly two thousand pounds sterling, *(140,000 UK pounds/200,000 US dollars today),* but Mary is not mentioned in his will either.

He is, however, the only uncle of hers who ever appears to have left any substantial legacy so perhaps he did renew the family bond with his grand-niece, the pair living near to each other in Liverpool, and she was later informally provided for out of this fund by the trustees of his estate, his daughter and son-in-law.

This remains speculation, and if Mary did come into new found wealth, there is certainly no evidence of any dramatic change of circumstance from the census records. If anything by 1891 things seems to have gone downhill.

Whether it was the trauma of losing their youngest son, a new found financial independence on Mary's part, or some other unknown factor, the dynamics of her relationship with the elder John Millward appeared to have changed, for the worse, and by 1891, the couple were living apart, though still both in the city of Liverpool, Mary lodging with friends in Toxteth, and John doing likewise in the Vauxhall Road district with their sixteen year old daughter Mary, claiming to be widowed, though this is a double lie, as quite besides Mary being alive and well a mile or so away, the couple had never in fact married.

It seems this was another family rift destined to remain unhealed. A further eight years on from this, in 1899, John Millward died, living alone in dank lodgings just around the corner from where he had been recorded with daughter Mary in 1891, and still eking out a living as a Clerk or Shorthand Writer. His end was a sad one indeed, his home part of a row of houses condemned for demolition the very same year by the city's Chief Medical Officer.

In his report he described it as one of the most unsanitary streets in all of Liverpool, with dilapidated buildings more than a hundred years old, overcrowded, saturated in filth, in a ruinous condition, with little sanitation, and a mortality rate running nearly three times higher than elsewhere in the city of Liverpool. Poignantly he added:

[62]

Built back to back on top of each other, very little sunlight or air could get in the houses, and the plants the corporation supplied to the poor people, for the window boxes there, just withered and died.

Unsurprisingly, John Millward had been in ill health in these poor surroundings. Suffering a stroke, had subsequently gone undiscovered for days. After post mortem on his body, the City Coroner recorded his cause of death in the official register as follows:

Apoplexy, accelerated by exposure to cold, due to having lain uncovered on the floor of his room, two nights previous.

His daughter Mary no longer appears to have been living with him, and unable to trace any relatives, the coroner was forced to guess an age of forty-seven for the death certificate, though he was in reality considerably older, and nearer sixty-three at the time.

Typical Victorian slum housing at Eldon Street, Liverpool, childhood home of John Lennon's paternal grandfather Jack Lennon.

Liverpool Records Office

Slum conditions in a one room lodging at Eldon Street, photographed in the early 20th century. John Lennon's great-grandfather, John Millward, born in the stately surroundings of Dolben Hall, ended his days in much reduced circumstances, in similar settings.

Liverpool Records Office

However unlucky life had proved for him in other respects, John Millward, with his partner Mary, sixteen years his junior, had seemingly always at least been blessed with youthful looks. When he had suffered his gunshot accident the local reports had likewise described him with the appearance of a *'young man'* despite him being near to thirty-seven even then.

How his *'widow'* Mary felt about his passing we do not know. Perhaps as a result of the not inconsiderable obstacles she had faced in her life from a young age, she had, by all accounts, matured into a powerful and head strong woman in her own right, who, according to the account of Lennon biographer Bob Spitz, was highly opinionated, a fluent Welsh speaker, who refused to speak English, labeling it the *'Devil's Tongue'*. Spitz does not quote his source on this, but certainly most of her Morris family in Wales were recorded as bilingual on the census records, and her Bridge relatives as speakers of Welsh only.

Her separation from her husband also seems to have led her to re-embrace the religion they had both grown up in, Mary now regularly attending the local Liverpool branch of the Welsh Calvinist Methodist church, as she would for much of the rest of her life.

In some ways, her own bitter life experiences, rather than soften her attitudes to others, appears to have hardened them. The account of John Lennon's sister, Julia Baird, recalls how, when her youngest daughter married a Catholic, she took the extraordinary move of disowning her as dead, nailing a black wreath onto her door, and refusing to ever again meet or speak with her.

The Welsh Calvinistic Methodist Church, Princes Street, Toxteth, Liverpool. Mary Elizabeth Morris/Millward, John Lennon's great-grandmother, was a regular member of the congregation here.

Undoubtedly there is some truth in this tale. Youngest daughter Harriet Millward is recorded as marrying an Irish Catholic, Patrick Joseph Matthews, from County Louth, in 1903. The pair in fact married in a Protestant church, perhaps a futile gesture to try and placate her mother's wrath at the mixed union.

In fact, parish records reveal Mary's only surviving son, George Millward, had also married into a Catholic family, two years earlier, his wife Catherine Higgins, being the daughter of Patrick Higgins, an Irish Tailor. Both these branches of the Millward family later emigrated, with their children, as far away from Liverpool as possible, beginning a new life together in New Zealand, in 1910, so once again a family rift in Mary Elizabeth's life appears to have been left permanently unhealed.

[64]

The overt prejudice towards Liverpool's Catholic population, also clearly shared by some of Lennon's Northern Irish Gildea ancestors, may appear quite shocking to us today, though it must be kept in mind these were attitudes very much borne of the times and environment, and far from uncommon then. It is interesting nevertheless to speculate whether this strong tradition of Ultra-Protestantism, and Anti-Catholicism, on both sides of John Lennon's mother, Julia Stanley's family, influenced their treatment of John's father Alfred Lennon, himself from a thoroughly Irish Catholic background?

Certainly, Julia's own sister, Mimi, appears to have been imbibed with some of the same views as her grandmother, as late as 1975 making clear to John her displeasure, at what she viewed as the 'branding' of his second son Sean, with an Irish Gaelic name.

Marriage of John Millward and Mary Elizabeth Morris's son, George Gordon Millward, Liverpool, in August 1901, his sister Harriet as a witness. George and Harriet both married into Irish families and immigrated with their spouses and children to New Zealand, where Mimi and John visited them at the height of Beatlemania.
Liverpool Record Office Reference Number: 283 NIC/3/106

John with his aunt Mimi and Mimi's cousin Thomas George Matthews (*30 Jan 1911-27 Jan 1993*), son of Harriet Catherine Ellenor Millward (*28 Aug 1877 - 11 May 1933*) and her husband Joe Matthews, an Irish Catholic from Dunleer, County Louth. The widowed Mimi and this unmarried cousin enjoyed a brief romantic attachment and for a time she lingered in New Zealand, after the Beatles tour of 1964, considering marriage.

[65]

Whether they initially met as near neighbours in Toxteth in the 1880s, and were childhood sweethearts, or romance only developed later in adult life, Mary's eldest daughter, Annie Jane Millward, and George Stanley, John's grandparents, did not rush into married life together either. Their first child, a daughter Charlotte Alice Stanley, was born in the summer of 1899, only to sadly pass away aged six months. She was followed by the only son ever born to the couple in the spring of 1903, George Ernest Stanley, junior, named for his father, who was also sadly lost to the family at just a few months of age

It may seem hypocritical perhaps, that Mary Elizabeth Millward would disown two of her children for marrying Catholics, whilst at the very same time her eldest daughter was technically *'living in sin'* with a man, and having children out of wedlock, until her own history in that regard is taken into account. Perhaps in this instance Annie's mother found herself less able to pass judgment on one of her children, having never been married herself. The fact George Stanley was at least from a middle-class Protestant background, with an uncle in the Orange Order to boot, must surely also have helped in some respect, given her clearly displayed views and prejudices on that subject.

Either way it would not, in the final eventuality, be until a full seven months after the birth of the couple's third child together, Mary Elizabeth Stanley, John's aunt Mimi, named for her powerful Welsh matriarch grandmother, (some would say fittingly so, born with a personality, seemingly very much in her mold), that the couple finally took the plunge and tied the knot, walking down the aisle in the November of 1906, by which time both were well in their early thirties. It is an irony perhaps that Mimi, the aunt who would later most strongly chastise her younger sister, John's mother Julia, for having children outside of marriage, was, in actual fact, herself born outside of wedlock.

The relative lateness of the couple's marriage may be attributable to the fact George Stanley had followed his father into a life on the sea, working as both a Boatswain and Sail Maker on the sea going ships, and as such would have only ever occasionally have been back in port for short stints. George and his father were also reputedly keen musicians, both playing the banjo, and it is likely this was a skill picked up at sea, where sailors shanty's such as *Maggie Mae,* which John later learned from his mother Julia, and eventually made its way on to the Beatles *Let It Be* album, were a staple favourite, echoing round the walls of many a crowded Liverpool dock pub at closing time, filled with men on their shore leave.

Baptism of Mary Elizabeth *'Mimi'* Stanley, St James, Toxteth, May 1906, the formidable and head strong eldest aunt who would raise John Lennon for much of his childhood.

Liverpool Record Office Reference Number: 283 JAM/2/7

After marriage, Annie and George Stanley were blessed with a further four children, all girls. The first, born in 1908, was named Elizabeth Jane, for George's mother Elizabeth Jane Stanley/Gildea, no doubt in recognition of the fact Annie had been allowed to name their elder girl, Mimi, after her own mother. Elizabeth was later known as *'Betty'*, *'Liz'*, or *'Mater,'* to younger members of the family. She appears aged three years old, with her mother and elder sister, on the census of 1911, at 36 Lydia Ann Street, Toxteth, again just a street or so away from the respective Gildea and Millward family homes.

[66]

The third child was born later the same year of the census, 1911, and given her mother's name Annie. She would be later known as *'Nanny'* to her nieces and nephews, including the young John Lennon. For her middle name she was given *'Georgina'* the female version of her father's name, though this would later be tinged with irony, as again according to Julia Baird's account of the family, on his eventual return to shore, George Stanley all but disowned her, believing her a *'changeling'* infant due to her deep red hair, and forever treating her distantly from then on.

The Stanley family, 1911 census, form filled out and signed by John Lennon's grandmother Annie Stanley, husband George Stanley, as so often the case, temporarily away from the family home, being recorded that year, working as a Boatswain, on a merchant ship docked in London.

Crown Copyright, Class: RG14; Piece: 22202

This would not be the case for his next daughter, the couple's fourth child. Despite also having red hair John Lennon's mother Julia, or *'Judy'* as she would be known to her siblings, was a vivacious and joyful child and, in contrast to her sister, soon became a firm favourite with their father. Two years later the family were completed with the birth of final daughter, Harriet, or *'Harrie'* Stanley, again a redhead, named for an aunt, her mother's youngest sister Harriet Millward in New Zealand, who by now was well into starting her own large family there.

With father George away at sea, and no brothers, the five Stanley sisters grew up for the most part in an all-female environment, learning to be independent, head strong and firm minded ladies from both their mother and grandmother, who had by now, in her old age, moved in with the Stanleys at their latest home, a ground floor apartment in Toxteth's Berkley Street.

Eldest sister Mimi became a particularly dominant force within the family dynamic, as she would remain for most of their lives, and when father George left the merchant service, in the autumn of 1922, at the age of forty eight, finding alternate work for himself on shore as a Digger for the Liverpool & Glasgow Salvage Association, she soon found herself in constant conflict with him.

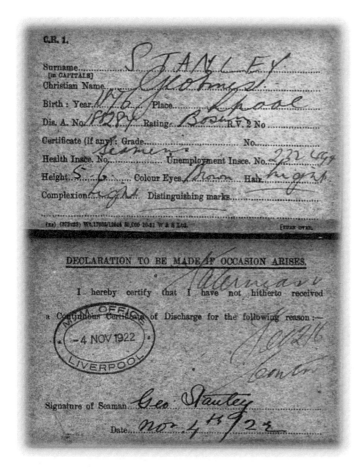

Naval Rating Card of John Lennon's grandfather, George Ernest '*Pop*' Stanley, who, like so many Liverpool men, spent much of his working life away from the home '*married to the sea*'. *Crown Copyright*

Youngest daughters Julia and Harrie, still just eight and six respectively, were more accepting of the sudden presence of a father figure in the home, who they affectionately nicknamed *'Pop'*. Clashes or not, none of George Stanley's daughters were in any great hurry to leave the family home, and it is ironic in fact that the two daughters he faced most difficulties with the headstrong eldest Mimi, and Annie the neglected middle child, were the last to leave him, neither marrying until well into their thirties.

The first daughter to leave the family home and perhaps the only one whose marriage was fully approved of by their father, was Elizabeth Stanley, who married at the age of twenty-four to thirty-seven-year-old Charles Molyneaux Parkes, a retired Royal Marines Captain, and a veteran of the First World War. The next to marry, youngest daughter Harrie, shortly before her twentieth birthday, in 1936, would create a minor scandal herself, in age before mixed culture marriages were the norm, with her choice of husband, Ali Hafez, a twenty-one-year-old Egyptian Engineering Student, moving with him and their daughter, Leila, to his home in Cairo shortly after.

Julia Stanley had meanwhile long been courting a man even more unsuitable in her father's eyes. She had first met the dashing young Fred Lennon on an outing to Liverpool's Sefton Park, when they were both still teenagers. He had impressed her with his quick and ready wit, responding to her criticism of his choice of head wear by promptly flinging the offending item into the park lake. Unlike Julia, her family were not so enamoured by the glib, dark haired, five-foot three lothario, who's very working class Irish roots, in one of the roughest parts of Toxteth, was neither what they expected of wished for in an ideal suitor for their favourite daughter.

Mary Elizabeth Stanley/Smith (1906-1991), the eldest daughter of George '*Pop*' Stanley and his wife Annie Jane Millward. She would exert a powerful and constant influence on the lives of her family, in particular John Lennon, the favoured nephew she took guardianship of at six years of age.

Often portrayed in biopics as a one-dimensional cold authoritarian character, Mimi was in fact a complex and fascinating individual, who enjoyed at least three of four serious romantic attachments in her life.

Digital Artwork based on an original photo taken by a fan at Mimi's home, Sandbanks, Poole, Dorset 1980s

Like Julia's father George, Fred Lennon was a man of the seas, and was often away for long periods at a time, though the young couple would regularly meet up on his visits back to shore, taking long walks together hand in hand in the park where they had met, often with Julia's infant nephew in tow, Stanley Parkes, her sister Elizabeth's son

It was on one such occasion, shortly after Harrie Stanley and her husband had left for Cairo, and near a decade into their courtship, that responding to pressure from both Julia's parents to either make an honest woman of her, or leave her alone to move on and find a more suitable match, Fred Lennon announced to his incredulous mother Polly Lennon that he was off to get married, to a girl she had yet to be introduced to, or had any of his family for that matter.

Lending the money from his stunned mother for the registrar's fee, he whisked Julia Stanley off to Mount Pleasant Registry Office. There, with Fred's elder brother Sydney Lennon and his wife hastily, and somewhat reluctantly, drafted into act as their last-minute witnesses, on the early winter morning of 3rd December 1938, the couple took their vows and became man and wife.

How Julia's family felt about their sudden nuptials can only be guessed at, especially as, before long, their new son-in-law had moved in with them at the latest Stanley family home in Newcastle Road, Wavertree, just around the corner from the Bluecoat Institute where he had spent his school days.

Any tensions were at least short lived, Pop, who had clearly favoured the later of the two options they had given their daughter, had arranged a two-year naval posting, intended to keep Fred as distant from Julia as possible, and as a result newlywed Fred was back off again to sea within days of their marriage, and soon busier than ever on the outbreak of the Second World War, in September 1939.

[69]

It was whilst on another of his regular, always eventful, shore leaves, in the opening months of 1940, at No.9 Newcastle Road, that Julia would fall pregnant with the first and only child to the marriage, born nine months later at the height of the German Blitz on the city of Liverpool, on the night of 9th October 1940, and patriotically named by his mother, as John Winston Lennon.

The Lake, Sefton Park, where John Lennon's teenage parents Alfred Lennon and Julia Stanley first met.

Ancestry of John Winston Ono Lennon

Patrick Lennon

Elizabeth

James McConville

Bridget Torley

Rodger Maguire

Bridget /Farley Farelly

William Henry Stanley

Elizabeth Miller

Charles Gildea

Ann Rogers

Thomas Millward

Jane Williams

William Morris

Ann Roberts

James Lennon
b: County Down, Ireland (Circa 1829)
m: 29 Apr 1849 in St. Anthony's....
d: 08 Jun 1898 in 12 Caradoc Road,...

Jane McConville
b: May 1831 in Newry, County....
d: 29 Jan 1869 in 31 Eldon Place,....
Occupation: Housekeeper

James Maguire
b: May 1840 in Whitewood, Nobber....
d: West Derby, Liverpool,....
Occupation: Horse Keeper

Mary Porter
b: 1845 in Liverpool, Lancashire,....
d: 1882 in West Derby, Liverpool,....
Occupation: Dress Maker

William Henry Stanley
b: 10 Dec 1846 in Birmingham,....
m: 14 Oct 1868 in St George....
Occupation: Solicitor's Clerk/Book....

Elizabeth Jane Gildea
b: 1846 in Drumragh, Omagh,....
d: 1916 in Toxteth Park, Liverpool,....

John Millward
b: Dolben Hall, Bontnewydd, St....
d: 16 Dec 1899 in 24 Smithfield,....
Occupation: Attorney's Writing....

Mary Elizabeth Morris
b: Apr 1851 in Berth y Glyd....
d: 11 Apr 1932 in 71a Berkley Street....

John 'Jack' Lennon
b: 12 Jan 1855 in Liverpool,
Lancashire, England
m: 27 Jan 1915 in West Derby
Register Office, Liverpool, Lancashire,
England
d: 03 Aug 1921 in 27 Copperfield
Street, Toxteth Park, Liverpool,
Lancashire, England

Mary 'Polly' Maguire
b: 20 Nov 1871 in West Derby,
Liverpool, Lancashire, England
d: 30 Jan 1949 in 27 Copperfield
Street, Toxteth Park, Liverpool,
Lancashire, England
Occupation: Laundress

George Ernest Stanley
b: 22 Aug 1874 in 120 Salisbury
Street, Everton, Liverpool, Lancashire,
England
m: 19 Nov 1906 in St Peter's,
Liverpool, Lancashire, England
d: 02 Mar 1949 in Smithdown Road
Hospital, 126 Smithdown Road,
Liverpool, Lancashire, England
Occupation: Errand Boy/Sailor &
Boatswain (Merchant Navy)

Annie Jane Millward
b: 21 Jun 1873 in "The Bear and Billet",
94 Lower Bridge Street, Chester,
Cheshire, England
d: 24 Apr 1941 in 9 Newcastle Road,
Wavertree, Liverpool, Lancashire,
England
Occupation: Seamstress

Alfred Lennon
b: 14 Dec 1912 in 27 Copperfield
Street, Toxteth Park, Liverpool,
Lancashire, England
m: 03 Dec 1938 in Mount Pleasant
Register Office, Liverpool, Lancashire,
England
d: 01 Apr 1976 in Brighton, Sussex,
England
Occupation: Merchant
Seaman/Waiter/Cook

Julia Stanley
b: 12 Mar 1914 in 8 Head Street,
Toxteth, Liverpool, Lancashire,
England
d: 15 Jul 1958 in Menlove Avenue,
Liverpool, Lancashire, England
Occupation: Cinema Attendant

John Winston Ono Lennon
b: 09 Oct 1940 in Liverpool Maternity
Hospital, Liverpool, Lancashire,
England
d: 08 Dec 1980 in New York, New
York, USA
Occupation:
Musician/Poet/Author/Artist

Ancestry of John Lennon's Paternal Grandfather John 'Jack' Lennon

John 'Jack' Lennon

b: 12 Jan 1855 in Liverpool, Lancashire, England
m: 27 Jan 1915 in West Derby Register Office, Liverpool, Lancashire, England
d: 03 Aug 1921 in 27 Copperfield Street, Toxteth Park, Liverpool, Lancashire, England
Occupation: Railway Clerk/Miller's Book Keeper/Brewer's Clerk/Grain and Sugar Warehouseman/Shipping & Freight Clerk

James Lennon

b: County Down, Ireland (Circa 1829)
m: 29 Apr 1849 in St. Anthony's Chapel, Scotland Road, Liverpool, Lancashire, England
d: 08 Jun 1898 in 12 Caradoc Road, Seaforth, Liverpool, Lancashire, England
Occupation: Merchant Warehouseman/Cooper/Warehouse Porter/Tram Car Company Manager, Proprietor & Owner

Patrick Lennon

b: County Down, Ireland
Occupation: Farmer

Elizabeth

b: County Down, Ireland

Jane McConville

b: May 1831 in Newry, County Down, Ireland
d: 29 Jan 1869 in 31 Eldon Place, Liverpool, Lancashire, England
Occupation: Housekeeper

James McConville

b: County Down, Ireland (Circa 1810)
d: Liverpool, Lancashire, England (Between 1851-61)
Occupation: Engineer

Bridget Torley

b: County Down, Ireland (Circa 1811)
d: Jun 1882 in Everton, Liverpool, Lancashire, England
Occupation: Servant

Ancestry of John Lennon's Paternal Grandmother Mary 'Polly' Maguire

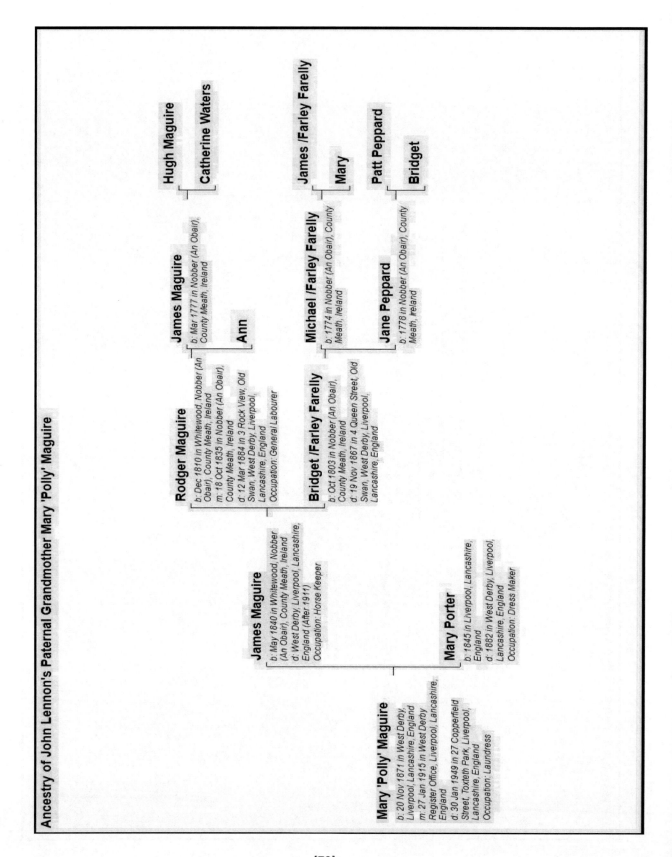

Hugh Maguire

Catherine Waters

James /Farley Farelly

Mary

Patt Peppard

Bridget

James Maguire
b: Mar 1777 in Nobber (An Obair),
County Meath, Ireland

Ann

Michael /Farley Farelly
b: 1774 in Nobber (An Obair), County
Meath, Ireland

Jane Peppard
b: 1778 in Nobber (An Obair), County
Meath, Ireland

Rodger Maguire
b: Dec 1810 in Whitewood, Nobber (An
Obair), County Meath, Ireland
m: 18 Oct 1835 in Nobber (An Obair),
County Meath, Ireland
d: 12 Mar 1884 in 3 Rock View, Old
Swan, West Derby, Liverpool,
Lancashire, England
Occupation: General Labourer

Bridget /Farley Farelly
b: Oct 1803 in Nobber (An Obair),
County Meath, Ireland
d: 19 Nov 1867 in 4 Queen Street, Old
Swan, West Derby, Liverpool,
Lancashire, England

James Maguire
b: May 1840 in Whitewood, Nobber
(An Obair), County Meath, Ireland
d: West Derby, Liverpool, Lancashire,
England (After 1911)
Occupation: Horse Keeper

Mary Porter
b: 1845 in Liverpool, Lancashire,
England
d: 1882 in West Derby, Liverpool,
Lancashire, England
Occupation: Dress Maker

Mary 'Polly' Maguire
b: 20 Nov 1871 in West Derby,
Liverpool, Lancashire, England
m: 27 Jan 1915 in West Derby
Register Office, Liverpool, Lancashire,
England
d: 30 Jan 1949 in 27 Copperfield
Street, Toxteth Park, Liverpool,
Lancashire, England
Occupation: Laundress

[73]

Ancestry of John Lennon's Maternal Grandfather George Ernest Stanley

William Stanley
b: (Circa 1784)
m: 27 Dec 1804 in Stroud,.....
d: Jul 1832 in William Street,....

Isabella Okey

William Henry Stanley
b: 1814 in St George, Southwark, Surrey, London, England
m: 08 Sep 1833 in St Anne's, Soho, Westminster, London, England
d: 30 Dec 1893 in Chilvers Coton, Warwickshire, England
Occupation: Carpenter/Solicitor's Clerk

John Miller
m: 18 Nov 1800 in St Mary's, Lambeth, Surrey, London, England

Elizabeth Abby

Elizabeth Miller
b: 1808 in Lambeth, Surrey, London, England
d: Warwickshire, England (Between 1851-61)

William Henry Stanley
b: 10 Dec 1846 in Birmingham, Warwickshire, England
m: 14 Oct 1868 in St George, Walton on the Hill Parish Church, Everton, Liverpool, Lancashire, England
Occupation: Solicitor's Clerk/Book Keeper/Warehouseman/Sailor/Mariner/Musician

William Gildea
b: Ireland (Circa 1770)
m: 24 Apr 1808 in Magheracross C....
d: Jan 1855 in Roscor,....

Charles Gildea
b: 1798 in Roscor, Magheracross, County Fermanagh, Ireland
m: Ulster, Ireland (Circa 1839)
d: 08 Mar 1861 in The Military Barracks, Drumragh, Omagh, County Tyrone, Ireland
Occupation: Commerical Office Clerk/Soldier 6th Dragoons & 99th Foot Regiment

Robert Rogers
Occupation: Book Keeper

Ann Rogers
b: County Tyrone, Ireland (Circa 1820)
d: 11 Nov 1906 in 6 Nile Street, Liverpool, Lancashire, England
Occupation: Lodging House Keeper

Elizabeth Jane Gildea
b: 1846 in Drumragh, Omagh, County Tyrone, Ireland
d: 1916 in Toxteth Park, Liverpool, Lancashire, England

George Ernest Stanley
b: 22 Aug 1874 in 120 Salisbury Street, Everton, Liverpool, Lancashire, England
m: 19 Nov 1906 in St Peter's, Liverpool, Lancashire, England
d: 02 Mar 1949 in Smithdown Road Hospital, 126 Smithdown Road, Liverpool, Lancashire, England
Occupation: Errand Boy/Sailor & Boatswain (Merchant Navy)

Ancestry of John Lennon's Maternal Grandmother Annie Jane Millward

John Millward

Robert Millward
b: 1756 in Faenol Fawr, Glascoed,......
m: May 1736 in St Asaph, Flintshire,.....
d: Feb 1831 in Bodelwyddan, St....

Alice (Catherine) Jones

Thomas Millward
b: 1787 in Bodelwyddan, St Asaph, Flintshire, Wales
m: 05 Mar 1830 in Denbigh, Denbighshire, Wales
d: Jan 1882 in Roe Street, Talar, St Asaph, Flintshire, Wales
Occupation: Professional Gardener & Carrier

Mary Jones

John Millward
b: Dolben Hall, Bontnewydd, St Asaph, Flintshire, Wales (Circa 1834)
d: 16 Dec 1899 in 24 Smithfeld Street, Liverpool, Lancashire, England
Occupation: Attorney's Writing Clerk/Clerk In Law Stationers Office/Lawyer's Clerk/Merchant's Clerk/Gentleman

Jane Williams
b: Nantglyn, Denbighshire, Wales (Circa 1804)
d: 1887 in Roe Street, Talar, St Asaph, Flintshire, Wales

Annie Jane Millward
b: 21 Jun 1873 in "The Bear and Billet" 94 Lower Bridge Street, Chester, Cheshire, England
m: 19 Nov 1906 in St Peter's, Liverpool, Lancashire, England
d: 24 Apr 1941 in 9 Newcastle Road, Wavertree, Liverpool, Lancashire, England
Occupation: Seamstress

Richard Morris
b: Penmachno, Carnarvon, Wales...
m: 22 Dec 1821 in Capel Garmon,.....
d: 30 Sep 1865 in Lletty Du,.....

Lynch Bridge

Elizabeth Bridge
b: 1795 in Tyn Twll, Meathebrwd,....
d: Jun 1854 in Lletty Du, Llanelian...

Catherine Sanders

William Morris
b: 1825 in Ty-brith Isa, Llanrwst, Denbighshire, Wales
m: 24 Dec 1847 in Llysfaen Parish Church, Llysfaen, Denbighshire, Wales
d: 09 Mar 1879 in Ty Celyn, Betws yn Rhos, Denbighshire, Wales
Occupation: Farmer (of 59 Acres at Ty Celyn, Betws yn Rhos)

Richard Roberts
b: 1795 in Tan Yr Allt Isa, Mochdre, Llandrillo yn Rhos, Denbighshire, Wales

John Roberts

Ann Jones

Mary
b: St Asaph, Flintshire, Wales (Circa 1796)

Ann Roberts
b: 1827 in Tan Yr Allt Isa, Mochdre, Llandrillo yn Rhos, Denbighshire, Wales
d: Mar 1861 in Ty Celyn, Betws yn Rhos, Denbighshire, Wales

Mary Elizabeth Morris
b: Apr 1851 in Berth y Glyd, Llysfaen, Denbighshire, Wales
d: 11 Apr 1932 in 71a Berkley Street, Toxteth, Liverpool, Lancashire, England

Ancestry of Elizabeth Bridge

William Bridge

b: 1720 in (Circa)
d: 05 Sep 1802 in Dinas, Llanwnda,
Cearnarvonshire, Wales
Occupation: Gentleman & Copper Mine Owner,
Conway Denbighshire Wales (1759)

Reverend Richard Farrington

b: 1702 in Bridge Street, Chester, England
d: 16 Oct 1772 in Bath, Somerset, England
Occupation: B.A Jesus College, Oxford.....

Mary Farrington

b: 1733 in (Circa) Brimslade, Wiltshire, England
d: 29 Apr 1808 in Dinas, Llanwnda,
Cearnarvonshire, Wales

Mary Ellis

b: Cheltenham, Gloucestershire, England
d: 1750 in Dinas Dinoethwy, Llanwnda,
Cearnarvonshire, Wales

Lynch Bridge

b: 1765 in Tal-y-Cafn, Eglwysbach, Llanrwst,
Denbighshire, Wales
m: 05 Feb 1790 in St Peter's, Liverpool,
Lancashire, England
d: May 1847 in Tyn Twll, Meathebrwd, Llanrwst,
Denbighshire, Wales
Occupation: Gentleman(1787)/Mariner(Liverpool
1790)/Farmer (of Tyn Twll, Llanrwst 1792-1847)

Elizabeth Bridge

b: 1795 in Tyn Twll, Meathebrwd, Llanrwst,
Denbighshire, Wales
m: 22 Dec 1821 in Capel Garmon, Llanrwst,
Denbighshire, Wales
d: Jun 1854 in Lletty Du, Llanelian yn Rhos,
Denbighshire, Wales

Catherine Sanders

b: (Circa 1771)
d: Oct 1843 in Tyn Twll, Meathebrwd, Llanrwst,
Denbighshire, Wales

Paul McCartney

Like the Lennons, the McCartney family roots lie across the Irish Sea in the Emerald Isle. In December 2008 it was reported in various media sources that Paul McCartney's brother Mike had undertaken research into the family that suggested they were originally *McCarthys* who had relocated *en masse* around 1860 from Ireland to Galloway, West Scotland and then moved on again some time, a little later, to Liverpool.

Whilst my own research has not confirmed this or any Scottish link, it is certainly true that the family's earliest days in Liverpool do show them variously recorded as *McCarthy* and *McCartney*, sometimes with both forms recorded on the very same document, and only after a generation or so does the latter, more familiar, form become exclusive to them.

What is also clear is the McCartney ancestors made the move to Liverpool much earlier than 1860, being present in the city at least from October 1822, the date the first documentary evidence can be found placing them there.

This comes from the baptism, on the 27th of that month and year, of Paul and Mike McCartney's great-great-grandfather, James McCartney, at St Anthony's Roman Catholic Chapel, Liverpool, having been born in the city, eleven days earlier, to his parents, Labourer, James McCartney, and wife Ann Rooney.

[77]

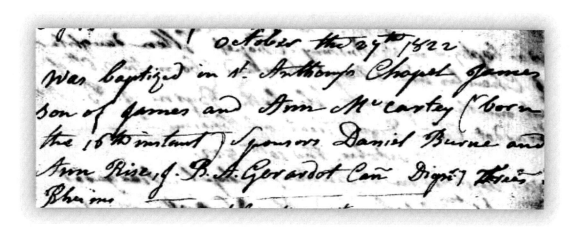

Earliest record of the McCartney family in Liverpool. Baptism of Paul McCartney's great-great grandfather, James McCartney, recorded here as McCartey, at St Anthony's Roman Catholic Church, in October 1822.
Liverpool Records Office Reference Number: 282 ANT/1/2

On the 1841 census, the first detailed census records to survive, the family, recorded in this instance as *MaCartny*, are found living at Rigby Place, Liverpool, close to the city's docks and just a short distance from the current site of the *Cavern Club* which would later be made so famous by the Beatles. James McCartney, junior, was recorded on this document as fifteen, He was in fact eighteen, but for reasons of bureaucracy census enumerators had been instructed that year to round adult ages down to the nearest five. At that time, he was following the trade of an Upholsterer's Apprentice. This document also provides the first firm evidence of Irish origin for the family, with both his parents clearly recorded as having been born in Ireland.

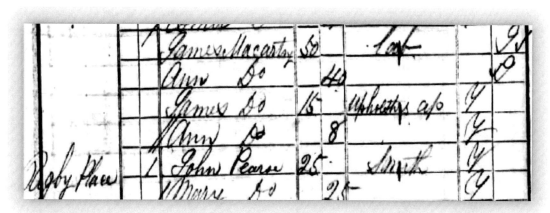

The McCartney family, Rigby Place, Liverpool 1841 Census. Paul McCartney's 3 x great-grandparents, James and Ann McCartney, *nee* Rooney, both recorded with 'I' for Ireland as their birthplace.
Crown Copyright, Class: HO107; Piece: 559; Book: 18; Enumeration District: 25; Folio: 20; Page: 33; Line: 3; GSU roll: 306941

Three years later, on the 14th of July 1844, at St Nicholas's Church, Liverpool, James McCartney, junior, was married, his occupation, like on the census, again recorded as an Upholsterer, having now completed his apprenticeship. His bride, Paul McCartney's great-great grandmother, was Rosanna Hughes. Both parties were recorded as minors on the marriage document, being under twenty-one, which again was not in fact strictly accurate, James would have been twenty-one at this time, though Rosanna certainly was a minor being only sixteen years of age at the time they wed.

Like James McCartney, Rosanna Hughes was part of Liverpool's fast growing Irish community, having been born in Ireland, and bought to Liverpool around the age of two with her parents James Hughes, a Labourer, and later a Provisions Merchant, and Alice McArdell, both Irish Roman Catholics.

Just where in Ireland the Hughes family came from is not recorded, and has so far proved impossible to trace with any real certainty, but the McCartney family's origin is given on the next census in 1851, by which time James McCartney, senior, widowed, had become an inmate at the Liverpool Union Workhouse, at Brownlow Hill. Here his place of origin was recorded as Newry, County Down, another strange coincidence in the Beatles story, also being the place of origin of John Lennon's ancestors, and at least one of Ringo Starr's ancestors too.

On the same 1851 census that found his father in such dire circumstance, James McCartney, junior, was himself recorded as missing, being temporarily away from his family home, his wife Rosanna, then living back with her parents, explaining his absence by recording on the form that her husband was *'In Ireland'*, presumably visiting McCartney relatives left behind there.

Paul McCartney's great-grandfather, James McCartney III, was the first child born to the newlywed James McCartney, junior, and Rosanna, seven months after their marriage, on 8th February 1845, in Liverpool. He was baptised eight days later at St Nicholas' Roman Catholic Church.

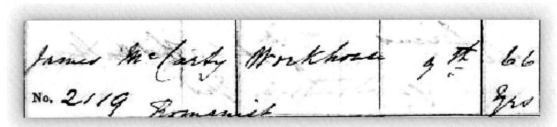

Entry in burial register of James McCartney, senior, Paul's 3 x great-grandfather. In 1851 he was recorded as an inmate of Liverpool Workhouse, and was sadly to remain there, where he died two years later, aged sixty-six, given the indignity of a pauper's burial in the unconsecrated section of the local C of E Churchyard, labelled a *'Romanist'*. On the 1851 Census he was recorded as *'McCartney'*, on his 1853 burial as *'McCarty'*, again showing the variability of spelling of the surname in Liverpool at this early period.
Liverpool Record Office Reference Number: 283 MTN/4/2/3

Paul McCartney's great-great grandmother, Rose (Rosanna) McCartney, aged twenty-three, at her parents, James & Alice Hughes' home, 35 Hodson Street, Liverpool, 1851 census, *'Husband in Ireland'* added to her entry. Her six-year-old son, James, Paul McCartney's great-grandfather, was later apprenticed to his uncle Patrick Hughes, also shown here, a Liverpool Plumber.
Crown Copyright, Class: HO107; Piece: 2179; Folio: 19; Page: 30; GSU roll: 87177-87178

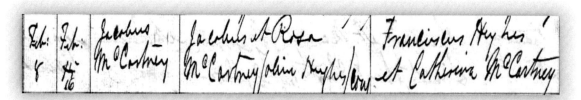

Baptism of Paul McCartney's great-grandfather, James McCartney III, recorded in Latin, February 1845, his mother's eldest brother, Francis Hughes as his godfather, and Catherine McCartney, his father's elder sister, as godmother. *Liverpool Record Office Reference Number: 282 NIC/1/3*

A further four children, two girls, Ann and Alice, would be born to them in 1847 and 1848 respectively, named for the couple's mothers, and then two more sons, Francis and Joseph, born in 1850 and 1858. Sadly, only the youngest brother Joseph, would survive alongside Paul's great-grandfather James, into adulthood, the other siblings all succumbing to various childhood disease and illnesses before any of them reached more than two years of age, an all too familiar characteristic of every Victorian working class areas across the land, where high infant mortality was a harsh, but accepted, reality of everyday life.

With large families, and high infant mortality, life was a harsh grind for the Victorian working class

Not long after youngest son Joseph's birth in 1858, Rosanna McCartney is recorded as being widowed. No burial can be found for her first husband James McCartney, junior, in Liverpool, so he may well have died away from the family home, perhaps again back in Ireland as he had been in 1851. Whatever the case, still just thirty years of age herself, on the 20th November 1859, Rosanna was remarried at St Anthony's Roman Catholic Church, Liverpool.

Her new husband was John Andrew Templeton, a twenty-seven-year-old Provisions Dealer, and a neighbour and employee of her late father James Hughes. Rosanna went on to have two further children with him, a son John Francis Templeton, a year on from the marriage in October 1860, and another, Thomas Templeton, a year on from that in the December of 1861.

[80]

The family is recorded together, Rosanna, her new husband and baby son, her two surviving McCartney sons from her first marriage, and her widowed mother Alice, living two doors from her parent's old home, at no.39 Hodson Street, Liverpool on the census taken in spring 1861. Paul's great-grandfather James McCartney, then fifteen, was recorded as an Apprentice Plumber. Rosanna would thereafter remain at this address, later being widowed again and remarrying for a third and final time, to a Patrick Needham, another Provisions Merchant, dying there as his wife, at the age of fifty-eight.

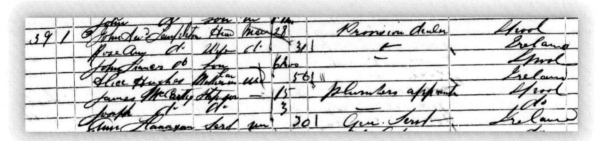

Paul McCartney's great-grandfather James McCartney, recorded as McCarthy, aged 15, at 39 Hodson Street, Liverpool, 1861. *Crown Copyright Class: RG 9; Piece: 2665; Folio: 24; Page: 44; GSU roll: 543009*

Hodson Street, Liverpool, early 20th century. Described in the December 15th 1853 *Liverpool Mercury*, as the *'most densely populated'* area of the city, occupied by what they deemed *'The very lowest class of Irish, in a most filthy state'*. Home to both a Ragged School for pauper children, and, due to the high rate of alcoholism amongst the residents, a Temperance Mission, this street, long since demolished, housed Paul McCartney's ancestors for much of the Victorian era. His origins lay very much in the city's Irish working-class tradition.

Liverpool Record Office

St Anthony's Roman Catholic Church, Liverpool. On Scotland Road at the heart of the Liverpool immigrant Irish community, this chapel is of great importance in the Beatles story, in the half century between 1820-70, hosting amongst others, the baptism of both Paul McCartney's great-great grandfather and grandfather, the baptism of Ringo Starr's great grandmother, and the marriage of John Lennon's great grandparents.

Three years on from the census, at the age of nineteen, James McCartney, now a fully qualified Plumber, was himself married, on 1st November 1864, to Elizabeth Williams, the seventeen-year-old daughter of a Liverpool Boiler Maker and Riveter, George Williams and his wife Jane Woolfall.

This blood link to the Woolfall family provides Paul McCartney with his longest traceable ancestry in the city of his birth, Liverpool. Jane's great-grandfather, Paul's 5 x great-grandfather, Abraham Woolfall, a Potter and Marble Polisher, was the first of Paul's ancestors to move there, from his place of birth in nearby Kirkby, in the opening years of the 1760s. In this he joins fellow Beatles, Ringo and George, who can all trace their ancestry in the city to at least the mid-18th century, though not John Lennon, whose earliest ancestors did not settle in the city until almost a century after his compatriots, in the late 1840s as refugees from the Irish Famine.

Unlike the McCartneys, Elizabeth and her Williams family were Protestants, and compromise was evidently reached, with the couple marrying in the Protestant Church of England, but all their children being baptised thereafter as Catholics.

The first child born to the couple, a year and one month after the marriage was a daughter, named Alice for her paternal grandmother, Alice Hughes, though who sadly did not survive.

Almost exactly a year on from this the couple's first son was born, Joseph, named for his paternal uncle, on 23rd November 1866 at Great Homer Street, Everton. This was Paul McCartney's grandfather, and he was duly baptised a fortnight later, like his sister had been, into the Catholic tradition, at the McCartney family's traditional place of worship, St Anthony´s Roman Catholic Church.

[82]

Baptism of Paul McCartney's grandfather Joseph, St Anthony's Roman Catholic Church, 23rd November 1866
Liverpool Record Office Reference Number: 282 ANT/1/8

The next census of 1871 finds the young Joe McCartney and his parents living back in Liverpool's Scotland Road district, at No.8 Bevington Street, a short distance from grandmother Rosanna's home, and coincidentally almost directly opposite John Lennon's sixteen-year-old grandfather John *'Jack'* Lennon and his family who were at that time living at Eldon Street.

James and Elizabeth McCartney went on to have a further six children after Joe's birth, five daughters and a son, born over the course of the next twenty-five years. The dates of birth show considerable gaps, and the census records help explain this apparent anomaly, by showing James McCartney, like so many Liverpool men before and after him, at some point abandoned his first trade as Plumber and Painter for the allure of a life on the sea in the merchant service, subsequently leaving his family at home alone for long periods of time.

This was recorded as the case on the next census of 1881 which finds James as Crewman on the SS *Mary Tatham*, a steam powered cargo ship built in Sunderland two years before. Merchant Naval records show James held the position of Ship's Fireman, and had been employed on the vessel since the 1st of January that year, having previously been a crewmate on the SS *Theresina*. The *Mary Tatham* was wrecked only a year later, off the coast of Japan, though if James was still crew at that time is not known.

Meanwhile, Elizabeth McCartney was recorded back at the family home in Liverpool with the couple's children, Paul McCartney's grandfather Joseph, fourteen, and his two younger sisters Mary, eight and Annie, two.

Interestingly the teenage Joe McCartney is in this early instance recorded as a Barber, though he would not go on to pursue this career path into adulthood, a decade later the 1891 census recording him as a Tobacco Grinder, the career, which he would follow the remainder of his life, as a Tobacconist, at Copes a local Liverpool firm.

By the time of the same 1891 census, sadly his mother Elizabeth had also been widowed, husband James McCartney having died only a few weeks before the census was taken, in the Liverpool Infirmary of a brain hemorrhage, at just forty-six years of age. Elizabeth was again pregnant at the time, and the couple's final child Ada McCartney was born just four months later on 31st August that year, tragically having never had the chance of knowing her father.

Elizabeth Williams/ McCartney, recently widowed, with her family on the 1891 census at 20 Holborn Street, Liverpool. Paul McCartney's Grandfather Joe, still living at home, aged twenty-four, recorded as a Tobacco Grinder. His sister Mary, eighteen, also employed in the same trade as a Cigar Maker.
Crown Copyright Class: RG12; Piece: 2991; Folio: 122; Page: 27

Elizabeth McCartney went on to remarry five years later, on 20th December 1896, at Christ Church, Kensington, Liverpool to Joseph Brewer, a Paver, himself a widower, but not before, a few months earlier, on 17th May, at this same church she had witnessed eldest son Joseph also get married. A few months short of his thirtieth birthday, like his father, he chose to take a Protestant girl for his wife, Florence *'Florrie'* Clegg.

Florence Clegg, paternal grandmother of Paul McCartney, later known to her grandchildren as *'Granny Mac'*, was the daughter of Paul Clegg, a Liverpool Fishmonger, and his third wife Jane Clague. The records show her father Paul, who died whilst she was still a child, was in fact also originally a Clague too, and his wife, who was twenty-two years his junior, possibly a distant cousin, though Paul and his family had changed the spelling of their surname shortly after moving to Liverpool from the Isle of Man, where both he and his wife were originally born, in Arbory and Douglas respectively.

A Victorian Fishmonger and Poulterer plies his trade, the occupation followed by Paul Clegg, Paul McCartney's Manx Liverpudlian great-grandfather.
London Illustrated News 1889

After their marriage, Paul McCartney's grandparents Joe and Florrie soon settled down to family life together, Joe, when not about his work as a tobacconist, a keen amateur musician, playing double bass in his works brass band, and on occasion the local Territorial Army band, eagerly steering and encouraging his children towards this pursuit too.

Unlike his own parents, Joseph McCartney chose not to baptise Florence and his children as Catholics and all eight of them, including Paul McCartney's father James, or '*Jim*', the fifth child born to the couple in 1902, were instead baptised in the various local Protestant churches around the family home in Fishguard Street, Everton. They also received Protestant schooling, which Joe McCartney evidently believed was of a better standard to the Catholic alternative on offer, that he himself had received.

If the Irish Catholic tradition appears to have temporarily died out in the McCartney family at the turn of the century with Paul's grandfather Joe, it was to receive a new injection of life on the wedding of Paul McCartney's father Jim in April 1941 to his mother Mary Patricia Mohin. Mary's family upbringing was very much traditional and Catholic, with both her parents coming, like the McCartney family, from Liverpool's Irish community.

Born on the 29th September 1909 at 2 Third Avenue, Fazakerley, Liverpool, Mary Mohin McCartney was the second of four children to her parents Owen Mohin, a Coal Merchant, and Mary Theresa Danher. Owen was originally a native of Tullynamalra, a small rural village near Lough Egish in County Monaghan, Ireland, where both his grandfather and his father Owen, senior, had been farmers of the land, on their own small holding, for the best part of a century. Owen was christened with the surname Mohan, but allegedly had the spelling changed for him on the arbitrary decision of a primary school teacher in the local village, who re-christened half the Mohans in his class as Mohin, to ease his own confusion. However, records show his father was also buried under this spelling, so this may not be strictly accurate. Whatever the truth of this tale, Owen certainly stuck to this latter spelling throughout his adult life!

Castleblayney, Co. Monaghan, Ireland, where Paul McCartney's great-grandparents Owen Mohin and Mary McGeogh were married in 1870, and where Paul himself was married, to second wife, Heather, in 2002.

One of nine children to his parents, and with two elder brothers set to inherit the land before him, Owen, or '*Ownie*' as he was affectionately known to his family, instead set out to make his own way in the world, leaving his home land, still a teenager, to seek his living across the water.

On this maternal branch of the McCartney family tree, ironically a Scottish link is provable, Owen and Mary's marriage on 24th April 1905 at St. Charles Roman Catholic Church, Toxteth Park, Liverpool, recording Owen's then address as Glasgow, and the 1901 census for Scotland, taken four years previous, showing him living and following his trade there.

[85]

Just what bought him to Liverpool and his future wife Mary Theresa can only be guessed at,but may well have been a business connection. The industrial hub of Liverpool would have been rich pickings for a Coal Merchant, and trade and traffic between the two great ports of Glasgow and Liverpool was heavy and frequent.

Owen's new bride Mary Theresa Danher, was herself native to the city of Liverpool, being born there on the 1st April 1877. Like the McCartneys she was the product of a mixed marriage, her father John Danher, an Irish Catholic, born in Limerick City, her mother Jane Baines, an English Protestant from Dudley, the daughter of John Baines, a Black Country Tailor and his wife Elizabeth Bowater, a Dressmaker and Tailoress.

Like the McCartney's, the Danher's reached the same familiar compromise of marrying in the Protestant church but baptising their children, and their long marriage was blessed with fourteen of them, into the Catholic tradition. The census records show Mary's father John Danher following various trades, amongst them Gas Fitter, Gas Meter Maker and finally Tallow Chandler.

A Victorian Tallow Chandler at work molding candles, one of several trades recorded for Paul McCartney's great-grandfather, John Danher.

In another re-occurring pattern on the McCartney family tree, it seems his surname also changed over time being originally spelt in Ireland and his early days in Liverpool with an extra 'a' as *'Danaher'*

After their marriage Paul's maternal grandparents, Owen Mohin and Mary Danher settled down into a terraced home in Liverpool's Fazakerly region, where four children were born to them Wilfred in 1908, Mary, Paul McCartney's mother, in 1909, Agnes in 1915, who sadly died just short of her third birthday, and finally Owen, junior, in 1917, who was known as Bill to his family, perhaps to ease possible confusion with his father. Little is known of their early life there, though in March 1913, Owen sold a Piano and a gramophone second hand in the *Liverpool Echo*, so perhaps in this there is a hint of music as a favoured hobby. Around the time of his last child's birth in May 1917 he appears in the *Liverpool Daily Post* selling off several horses, and other related equipment having decided to bring his business into the modern era switching to *'Heavy Motor Traction'*.

[86]

Tragically Mary Danaher/Mohin died whilst her children were all still very young, shortly after the end of the First World War, in the opening days of 1919. Not long after, Owen returned to Ireland where he was remarried just under two years later to Rose Lawless of Dundalk. On their return to Liverpool, his children did not warm to their new Step-Mother, and Paul's mother Mary, still in her teens, left the family home, to train as a Nurse and Midwife.

1.	2.	3.	4.	5.	6.	7.	8.	9.	10.
Owen Mohin	head	29		married					Coal Merchant 598
Mary Mohin	wife		30	married					coal dealer
Wilfred Mohin	son	2½							asst coal hawker
Mary Mohin	daughter		1½						housekeeper

Paul McCartney's mother Mary, aged eighteen months, with her parents and older brother Wilfred, recorded at Number 2, Third Avenue, Fazakerley, Liverpool, 1911.
Crown Copyright Class: RG14; Piece: 22350

With advancing years, her father Owen became ever more drawn into the familiar vices of so many working-class men of the era, the temporary relief from drudgery offered through drink and gambling, and as a result he also suffered a premature death, in considerably reduced circumstance, aged fifty-three, whilst visiting his wife's relatives in Ireland.

Though his own relatives in Monaghan lived a mere twenty miles away from new wife Rose's in Dundalk, it appears he had long lost all contact with the family he had left there, his youngest brother Peter reportedly searching for him in Liverpool as late as the 1950s, in the belated hope of renewing their fraternal bond, unaware his elder sibling had long been dead for twenty years by that point.

Out on her own in the world, her mother and father both now gone, Mary Mohin soon became a much-respected member of her profession. It was however, then as now, not a profession which pays anywhere near as well as it should, and unable to afford a home of her own, she took lodgings with a local couple called Harry and Ginny Harris in West Derby, Liverpool.

Ginny was a year younger than Mary, and the two soon became firm friends. So close Mary was frequently invited to Ginny's mother's home, the McCartney household in Scargreen Avenue, Norris Green, Ginny in fact being born as Jane McCartney, the youngest child of Joseph McCartney and Florrie Clegg.

It was whilst on one such visit, during an air raid shortly after the outbreak of the Second World War, Mary met her future husband, Ginny's elder brother, Jim McCartney, by now in his late thirties, and a successful Cotton Merchant, as well as a keen amateur Musician with his own band. The pair fell in love, and after a brief courtship, tied the knot the following year, on 15th April 1941 at St Swithin's Roman Catholic Church, Gill Moss.

Paul McCartney, the child who would inherit the musical leanings of both father and grandfather, and go on to be one of the most commercially successful Musical Artists of modern times, was born to them a little more than a year on, christened James Paul McCartney, for his father, with younger brother Peter Michael McCartney, known as Mike, coming along to complete the family a little over eighteen months later.

[87]

Ancestry of Paul McCartney

James McCartney
b: 08 Feb 1845 in Liverpool, Lancashire, England
m: 01 Nov 1864 in St Peter's, Walton on the....
d: 03 Mar 1891 in Liverpool Royal Infirmary....

Elizabeth Williams
b: 1847 in Birkenhead, Cheshire, England
d: 1915 in West Derby, Liverpool, Lancashire,
England

Paul /Clague Clegg
b: 1815 in Arbory, Isle of Man
m: 09 Jul 1863 in Liverpool Register Office....
d: 1879 in Everton, Liverpool, Lancashire,....

Jane Clague
b: 1837 in Douglas, Isle of Man
d: 1909 in Everton, Liverpool, Lancashire,
England

Owen Mohan
b: 1842 in Tullynamalra, Lough Egish, County....
m: 01 Mar 1870 in Chapel of Lattice....
d: 1903 in Tullynamalra, Lough Egish, County....

Mary McGeogh
b: 1847 in Drumgar, County Monaghan, Ireland
d: Tullynamalra, Lough Egish, County Monaghan,
Ireland (After 1911)

John /Danaher Danher
b: Limerick, County Limerick, Ireland (Circa 1841)
m: 25 Sep 1865 in St Mary's Catholic Chapel....
d: 13 Feb 1917 in 58 Leasowe Road, Wallasley....

Jane Baines
b: 13 May 1848 in Dudley, Worcestershire....
d: 28 Nov 1920 in 58 Leasowe Road, Wallasley.....

Joseph McCartney
b: 23 Nov 1866 in 2 Court, Great Homer Street,
Everton, Liverpool, Lancashire, England
m: 17 May 1896 in Christ Church, Kensington,
Liverpool, Lancashire, England
d: 1927 in West Derby, Liverpool, Lancashire,
England
Occupation: Barber

Florence Clegg
b: 02 Jun 1874 in 131 Breck Road, Everton,
Liverpool, Lancashire, England
d: 07 May 1945 in Liverpool, Lancashire, England

Owen /Mohan Mohin
b: 19 Jan 1880 in Tullynamalra, Lough Egish,
County Monaghan, Ireland
m: 24 Apr 1905 in St Charles Roman Catholic
Church, Toxteth Park, Liverpool, Lancashire,
England
d: 19 Aug 1933 in Blackrock, Dundalk, County
Louth, Ireland
Occupation: Coal Merchant

Mary Theresa Danher
b: 01 Apr 1877 in 13 Minto Street, Toxteth Park,
Liverpool, Lancashire, England
d: Jan 1919 in 19 Warbreck Moor, Fazakerley,
Liverpool, Lancashire, England

James McCartney
b: 07 Jul 1902 in 8 Fishguard Street, Everton,
Liverpool, Lancashire, England
m: 15 Apr 1941 in St Swithin's Roman Catholic
Church, Gill Moss, West Derby, Liverpool,
Lancashire, England
d: 18 Mar 1976 in 20 Beverley Drive, Gayton,
Wirral, Lancashire, England
Occupation: Cotton Salesman

Mary Patricia Mohin
b: 29 Sep 1909 in 2 Third Avenue, Fazakerley,
Liverpool, Lancashire, England
d: 31 Oct 1956 in Northern Hospital, Liverpool,
Lancashire, England
Occupation: Nurse, Matron, Midwife

James Paul McCartney
b: 18 Jun 1942 in Walton Hospital, Liverpool,
Lancashire, England
Occupation: Musician & Song Writer

[88]

Ancestry of Paul McCartney's Paternal Grandfather Joseph McCartney

Joseph McCartney

b: 23 Nov 1866 in 2 Court, Great Homer Street, Everton, Liverpool, Lancashire, England
m: 17 May 1896 in Christ Church, Kensington, Liverpool, Lancashire, England
d: 1927 in West Derby, Liverpool, Lancashire, England
Occupation: Barber

James McCartney

b: 08 Feb 1845 in Liverpool, Lancashire, England
m: 01 Nov 1864 in St Peter's, Walton on the Hill, Everton, Liverpool, Lancashire, England
d: 03 Mar 1891 in Liverpool Royal Infirmary, Liverpool, Lancashire, England
Occupation: Plumber/Painter/Seaman

Elizabeth Williams

b: 1847 in Birkenhead, Cheshire, England
d: 1915 in West Derby, Liverpool, Lancashire, England

James /McCartney McCarthy

b: 16 Oct 1822 in Liverpool, Lancashire, England
m: 14 Jul 1844 in St Nicholas, Liverpool, Lancashire, England
d: Whearabouts Unknown, Possibly Ireland (Between 1857-9)
Occupation: Upholsterer

Rosanna Hughes

b: Ireland (Circa 1828)
d: Mar 1886 in 39 Hodson Street, Liverpool, Lancashire, England

George Williams

b: 1827 in Liverpool, Lancashire, England
m: 04 Aug 1845 in St Nicholas, Liverpool, Lancashire, England
Occupation: Boiler Maker

Jane Woolfall

b: 1826 in Arley Street, Liverpool, Lancashire, England

James /McCartney McCarthy

b: Newry, County Down, Ireland (Circa 1787)
d: Mar 1853 in Liverpool Workhouse, Brownlow...
Occupation: Labourer

Ann Rooney

b: Ireland (Circa 1801)
d: Jan 1847 in Liverpool, Lancashire, England

James Hughes

b: Ireland (Circa 1793)
d: Nov 1853 in 35 Hodson Street, Liverpool...
Occupation: Labourer (1841)

Alice McArdell

b: Ireland (Circa 1805)
d: Feb 1870 in 39 Hodson Street, Liverpool...

William Williams

m: 18 Nov 1811 in Holy Trinity, Liverpool...
Occupation: Mariner

Hannah Craige

Thomas Woolfall

b: 10 May 1795 in Pitt Street, Toxteth...
m: 31 Dec 1817 in St Nicholas, Liverpool...
d: Nov 1860 in Liverpool, Lancashire, England

Mary Timpson

b: Lancashire, England (Circa 1800)
d: 1847 in Liverpool, Lancashire, England

Ancestry of Paul McCartney's Paternal Grandmother Florence Clegg

John /Clague Clegg

Robert /Clague Clegg
b: 1788 in Arbory, Isle of Man
m: 19 Dec 1807 in Arbory, Isle of Man
Occupation: Farmer

Elizabeth Comish

Thomas Clague
b: Isle of Man
Occupation: Farmer

Paul /Clague Clegg
b: 1815 in Arbory, Isle of Man
m: 09 Jul 1863 in Liverpool Register Office,
Liverpool, Lancashire, England
d: 1879 in Everton, Liverpool, Lancashire,
England
Occupation: Wheelwright/Millwright/Pattern
Maker/Fish Monger

Jane Clague
b: 1837 in Douglas, Isle of Man
d: 1909 in Everton, Liverpool, Lancashire,
England
Occupation: Fishmonger

Florence Clegg
b: 02 Jun 1874 in 131 Breck Road, Everton,
Liverpool, Lancashire, England
m: 17 May 1896 in Christ Church, Kensington,
Liverpool, Lancashire, England
d: 07 May 1945 in Liverpool, Lancashire, England

Owen /Mohan Mohin

b: 19 Jan 1880 in Tullynamalra, Lough Egish, County Monaghan, Ireland
m: 24 Apr 1905 in St. Charles Roman Catholic Church, Toxteth Park, Liverpool, Lancashire, England
d: 19 Aug 1933 in Blackrock, Dundalk, County Louth, Ireland
Occupation: Coal Merchant

Owen Mohan

b: 1842 in Tullynamalra, Lough Egish, County Monaghan, Ireland
m: 01 Mar 1870 in Chapel of Lattice, Castleblayney, County Monaghan, Ireland
d: 1903 in Tullynamalra, Lough Egish, County Monaghan, Ireland
Occupation: Farmer

Mary McGeogh

b: 1847 in Drumgar, County Monaghan, Ireland
d: Tullynamalra, Lough Egish, County Monaghan, Ireland (After 1911)

Ancestry of Paul's Maternal Grandmother Mary Theresa Danher

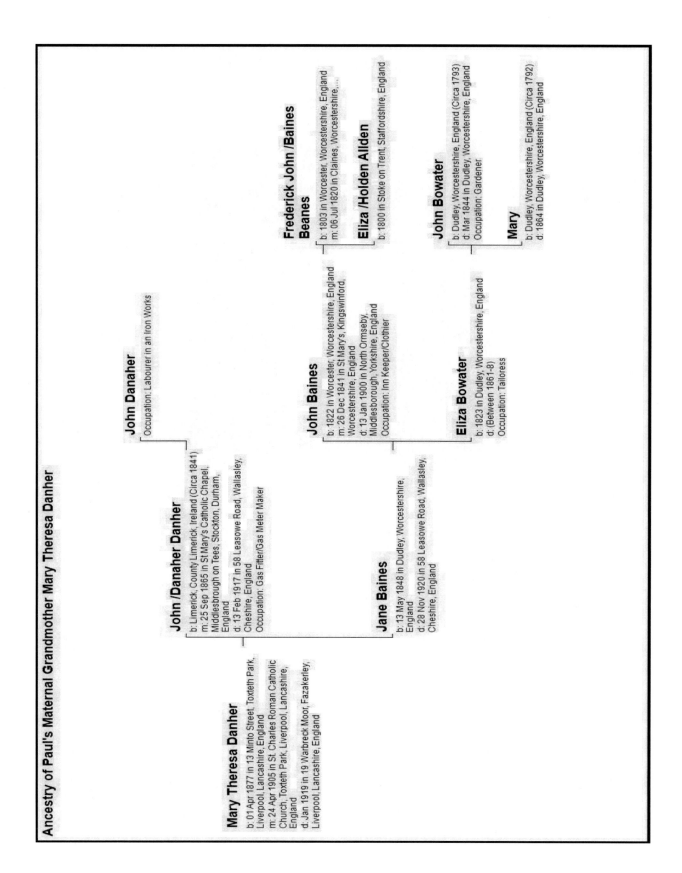

Mary Theresa Danher
b: 01 Apr 1877 in 13 Minto Street, Toxteth Park, Liverpool, Lancashire, England
m: 24 Apr 1905 in St. Charles Roman Catholic Church, Toxteth Park, Liverpool, Lancashire, England
d: Jan 1919 in 19 Warbreck Moor, Fazakerley, Liverpool, Lancashire, England

John /Danaher Danher
b: Limerick, County Limerick, Ireland (Circa 1841)
m: 25 Sep 1865 in St Mary's Catholic Chapel, Middlesbrough on Tees, Stockton, Durham, England
d: 13 Feb 1917 in 58 Leasowe Road, Wallasley, Cheshire, England
Occupation: Gas Fitter/Gas Meter Maker

John Danaher
Occupation: Labourer in an Iron Works

Jane Baines
b: 13 May 1848 in Dudley, Worcestershire, England
d: 28 Nov 1920 in 58 Leasowe Road, Wallasley, Cheshire, England

John Baines
b: 1822 in Worcester, Worcestershire, England
m: 26 Dec 1841 in St Mary's, Kingswinford, Worcestershire, England
d: 13 Jan 1900 in North Ormseby, Middlesborough, Yorkshire, England
Occupation: Inn Keeper/Clothier

Frederick John /Baines Beanes
b: 1803 in Worcester, Worcestershire, England
m: 06 Jul 1820 in Claines, Worcestershire,....

Eliza /Holden Allden
b: 1800 in Stoke on Trent, Staffordshire, England

Eliza Bowater
b: 1823 in Dudley, Worcestershire, England
d: (Between 1861-8)
Occupation: Tailoress

John Bowater
b: Dudley, Worcestershire, England (Circa 1793)
d: Mar 1844 in Dudley, Worcestershire, England
Occupation: Gardener

Mary
b: Dudley, Worcestershire, England (Circa 1792)
d: 1864 in Dudley, Worcestershire, England

George Harrison

Of the four Beatles, the Harrison family have roots most firmly entrenched in the city of Liverpool. The earliest Harrison that can be traced, George's 4 x great-grandfather, Robert Harrison, a farmer, was not actually Liverpudlian himself, though a Lancastrian nonetheless hailing from Warrington, twenty miles to the east. There he married his 24-year-old bride Sarah Orrett, a farmer's daughter from Rainford, in the early autumn of 1794. It was through the somewhat indirect route of her elder brother, Ralph Orrett, the Harrisons first came to be in the city of Liverpool.

Nine days before his sister's marriage, Ralph Orrett had also been married at St James' Church, Toxteth, to local girl Margaret Brownbill. Ralph and Margaret settled in the town of Liveprool, where her ancestors had lived for at least a century, and perhaps to be near, Robert and Sarah Harrison settled not far away from them in Eccleston. The couples clearly remained close, and visited often, naming children for each other and standing as godparents for each other.

At some point Ralph and Margaret's eldest child, daughter Elizabeth Orrett, began a romance with her first cousin, Robert and Sarah's eldest child, Anthony Harrison, a year her junior, falling pregnant to him, unwed, when she was twenty and he nineteen. The child, George Harrison's great-great grandfather, was born on the 9th October 1816, in the Orrett family home in West Derby, Liverpool. The new father Anthony Harrison left his family and set up home with his cousin and their newborn son, who was baptised six weeks after the birth, and named Robert, for his grandfather. A week later the couple, on the 1st of December 1816, the couple were married, in the same church where the bride's parents had been married two decades previous, St James, Toxteth, perhaps both moves calculated gestures intended to placate each side of the family.

[93]

This romance and marriage of *'kissing cousins'*, which first bought the Harrisons to Liverpool, appears to have proved a happy and enduring union, Anthony and Elizabeth settling down to a long-married life together in their new home, with a further ten children, born to them over the course of the next two decades. The various census records show Anthony Harrison employed as a Joiner and House Carpenter, a trade which in theory should have been in brisk demand in the fast-growing urban metropolis of Liverpool in the early and mid-19th century. Despite this, he was, however, twice recorded as going bankrupt in the 1840s.

Nevertheless, his sons duly followed him into the trade, eldest Robert evidently with a greater degree of success, being recorded with his own Carpenter and Joiner's business, an employer of two others, on the census of 1861. In another move emulating his father, Robert was also married young, a month after his nineteenth birthday, in the November of 1835, to Sefton born, Jane Shepherd, twenty-one. Together they set up home in the area around Old Swan and Stanley, West Derby, Liverpool, where the Harrisons would remain for the best part of the next century, and there themselves raised a large family, with a total of twelve children born to this marriage.

Robert and Jane Harrison's sixth child, and third son, Edward Harrison, born on 13th January 1848, at Etna Street, Stanley, was the great-grandfather of George Harrison. Unlike his father and grandfather, he did not follow into the Carpenter's trade, but was nevertheless still very much involved in carving out the rapidly emerging Victorian Liverpool urban landscape, finding an apprenticeship for himself, in his teenage years, as a Bricklayer and Stonemason.

Shortly before completing this, he was married, at the age of twenty, in Liverpool, to George Harrison's great-grandmother, Elizabeth Hargreaves, a seventeen-year-old Mancunian, her grandfather James Hargreaves, a Warehouse Porter and Carrier, having moved his family, including Elizabeth's father John, also a Porter, to Manchester, a decade before her birth, from nearby Haslingden, Lancashire, which had long been the Hargreaves family home.

Like father and grandfather before him, Edward Harrison was blessed with a long-lasting marriage and another large brood, this time consisting of no less than thirteen children. Fourth son, Henry Harrison, known to his family as *'Harry'*, George Harrison's grandfather, was born on 21st January 1882 at the family home 12 Queen Street, Old Swan.

[94]

A Victorian carpenter and joiner with his apprentice, the occupation followed by George Harrison's 3 x great-Grandfather Anthony Harrison, and his sons

Despite the loving and relatively prosperous family home into which he was born, Harry Harrison's early years, were not untouched by tragedy. A particularly bleak twelve months began for the family in the late spring of 1890, when Harry was still just eight years of age. Only days before mother Elizabeth was due to give birth to the family's eleventh child, a son Herbert, youngest daughter Clara Harrison died just short of her second birthday. Baby Herbert sadly was not to prosper either, and also died three months later. However tragic this double blow, in a time where high infant mortality was a harsh reality of life for most families, the next loss must have been particularly hard to bear. This was the death of Harry's elder brother, William Edward Harrison, at the age of eighteen, in a swimming accident. Edward, their father, gave evidence at the inquest, and the full tragic story was reported in the *Liverpool Mercury*:

23rd June 1891 - SAD DROWNING FATALITY: An inquest was held yesterday afternoon at the Stanley Arms Hotel by Mr. Brighouse, County Coroner on the body of William Harrison of Old Swan who drowned in a pit whilst bathing on Sunday morning, Edward Harrison, Stonemason, 12 Queen St, Old Swan, identified the deceased as his son, aged 18, who lived with him. He last saw him alive at 6.30am on Sunday when he left with a companion for a ramble. On hearing of the mishap, he went to Roby Park and helped to get his son out. He did not know if his son could swim. Edward Standard, Brass-finisher, of 37 Queen St, said he accompanied the deceased, when they got near the pit, at about 8-10 am, deceased said he would go in, he tried to dissuade him without success. Harrison dived in head first, coming up on his back and tried to call witness who reached out his shirt, which nearly touched him but, he appeared unable to grasp it. He sank again and never came back up. Witness ran for assistance as he could not swim. Police Sergeant Edgar said it was a dangerous pit, someone had drowned there some time ago. It was 60-70 yards away from the highway and close to a public footpath. Jury recorded a verdict of 'Accidental Death' and made a presentment, that the pit in question should be filled in or fenced off and a board put up that it was dangerous to bathers.

Sadly, William Harrison was just one of three young men to die in Liverpool that weekend alone from accidental drowning, in an era when health and safety was not the public concern it is today. Whatever their thoughts and feelings on this dreadful run of tragedies, the family evidently pulled together, and remained strong, two more sons born to Edward and Elizabeth after this, Harold Hargreaves Harrison and Richard Hargreaves Harrison, in 1892 and 1895 respectively, completing the family.
Harry Harrison, by now a teenager, had decided to follow his father into the Stonemason's trade,

[95]

eventually, in his twenties, becoming a Master Bricklayer in and around Liverpool. He met his future wife, eighteen-year-old Jane Thompson of Wavertree, George Harrison's grandmother, shortly before his 20th birthday and they were married the following year, in the summer of 1902, at her local parish church of Holy Trinity, Wavertree.

Marriage of George Harrison's paternal grandparents at Wavertree Parish Church 1902. Both parties were underage, legal age of marriage without parent's consent being 21 at the time, and were *'economical with the truth'*, each adding two years to their real age! *Liverpool Record Office Reference Number: 283 HTW/3/2*

From his paternal grandmother Jane, George Harrison inherited another colourful mix of ancestors. Her mother Annie Caley was born on the Isle of Man around 1856, so like Paul McCartney, George can claim some Manx ancestry through this great-grandmother. Jane's father James Davidson Thompson was a native-born Scotsman, from Kirkinner, in the far west of that country. He had moved with his family from Scotland, to Liverpool, at nine years of age, when his own father Archibald Thomson, a Fireman on a steam boat in Scotland, had found alternate work as an Engine Driver with the Liverpool Company Water Works. James eventually followed Archibald into both these trades once in Liverpool, working as both an Engine Driver and Fireman, though in his case on the local railways.

Though James Thompson himself, and both his parents, father Archibald, and mother Jane Duff, were born and raised in Scotland, their ultimate roots lay further afield, across the water in Ireland. The census records reveal Archibald's grandfather Andrew Thomson, George Harrison's 4 x great-grandfather, a Farmer, had originally been born in Ireland before moving to Scotland, as too had both his wife Jane Duff's parents. This is not entirely surprising, and reflects a long tradition of fluid movement of people back and forth from Western Scotland and Northern Ireland, which is not just a phenomenon of recent centuries, but millennia old, at one time the area being a united entity, the Gaelic Kingdom of the Dal Riada, which predated, and led to the birth of, the country of Scotland.

Nevertheless, despite this winding path of genes back to Ireland, through at least one ancestor, Archibald Thomson's mother, Jane Gray, George's 3 x great-grandmother, originally a native of Tyron, Dumfries, George does have strong roots within Scotland, which can be traced back at least to the early 1700s, with links to several West Scottish clans such as the McKelvies, Thorburns, Muirs and Kennedys, evident. These roots he shares with Ringo Starr, who claims Scottish ancestry on both mother and father's side, though ironically not with fellow Beatle Paul McCartney for whom Western Scotland has become his latter-day home, and for whom Scottish ancestry has often been claimed, though without, it appears, any foundation.

[96]

**Whithorn, Kirkinner, Scotland,
birthplace of George Harrison's great-grandfather
James Davidson Thompson, 1857.**
Photo R.H Dengate

After their marriage at the opening of the 20ᵗʰ century, George Harrison's grandparents, Harry and Jane Harrison, settled into a family home in Wavertree. George's father, Harold Hargreaves Harrison, their fourth child, was born to them there on 28ᵗʰ May 1909. He was named for his father's younger brother, Harold Hargreaves Harrison, who had tragically died ten weeks earlier, of nephritis, a congenital kidney disease, at the premature age of sixteen. He must have been a much loved, and much missed sibling, as two more of his brothers George and Edward Harrison, would also name sons for him that year, as a result George Harrison's father was one of three cousins in Liverpool, all roughly the same age, to bear this same family name in remembrance.

There is every indication that had it not been for one of the most momentous and tragic events of the century, Harry Harrison and his wife would have again repeated the pattern of long happy marriage, and bountiful children, which had blessed each successive generation of the Harrison family in the century since they had moved to Liverpool. Tragically it was not to prove so, when on August 4ᵗʰ 1914 the world was plunged headlong into turmoil, and dark days of conflict, with the outbreak of the First World War.

The thirty-two-year-old Harry Harrison, like so many men across the country, resolved to go along to the local recruitment office, to answer Lord Kitchener's call and pin his colours to the national mast, diligently volunteering as soon as he could to do his duty for '*King and Country*'. After training he was billeted, as a private, to the 1ˢᵗ Battalion of the Loyal North Lancashire Regiment and soon after was sent with them, across the channel to France, in the early spring of 1915. Tragically he was one of the estimated 880,000 British men whose lives were sacrificed in the course of the four-year long conflict, being killed fighting with his battalion, on Sunday 25ᵗʰ September, that same year 1915, on the first bloody day of the Battle of Loos. His son Harold, George Harrison's father, was still just six years old at the time. Ten years later as a teenager he would attempt to enter service himself, in the Royal Navy, but was prevented from doing so by his widowed mother Jane, still distraught at the painful memory of her husband's tragic loss.

British infantry advancing into a gas cloud at Loos, France, 25ᵗʰ September 1915, the day George Harrison's grandfather Harry Harrison was killed there, one of 489 men in his battalion of 650 to die that day, and one of approximately 16,000 British service men killed in the course of the two-week battle.
Imperial War Museum

[97]

Duly blocked from this path the young Harold Harrison instead found work for a time, still on the sea, but in the Merchant Service as a Ship's Steward on the White Star Line. It was while in the service, on shore leave, he met a local teenage shop assistant Louise French, and falling in love, they were soon after married, in 1930, when he was aged twenty-one, and she was nineteen.

Through his mother Louise, George's ancestral trail once again winds rapidly back to Ireland. Her father John French, was a native of Ferns, County Wexford, where had had been born in the 1870s, to James Darby French, a Farmer, and his wife Ellen Whelen.

Originally spelt Ffrench, the family has long and noble roots in Ireland, stretching back to the 12th century invasion of the land under the same Francophone Norman overlords, who at that time also held sway across the water in England and much of North West France. Though they may have originally been powerful land owning barons in Wexford, by the time of George's great-grandparents, this wealth and power had long since watered down to nothing, the family like many of the original Catholic Anglo-Irish ruling class, suffering terribly in the 16th century religious reformation, and ultimately being stripped of all their remaining lands and power in the following brutal 17th century subjection of the country by Oliver Cromwell's invading forces, after lending their support to the ill-fated Stuart monarchy in the Civil War.

By the mid-19th century the French family were no different from any of their neighbours, and James and Ellen were simple country Crofters and small holders, striving against the odds, to keep their land going, by then just a two acre plot, and constantly struggling to keep their family clothed and fed, during some of the toughest economic times ever seen in Ireland, during and immediately after the Great Famine, the worst disaster to ever hit the country, massively ravaging and depopulating the land. This they admirably managed until their deaths, in 1906 and 1907, respectively.

Ferns Castle, two kilometers from the French family farmstead at Corah, Wexford, was built shortly after the 12th Century Norman Conquest of the Medieval Irish Kingdom of Leinster, the event which first bought the Ffrench Family into Ireland. *Photo Mike Searl*

Shortly before this, James and Ellen French's children, including George's great-grandfather John, realising the family farmstead's days were ultimately doomed, and leaving their elder sister Eliza in charge of both farm and parents, set out to make their own way in the world. John crossed over the water to Liverpool, finding himself work as a Policeman in the opening years of the 20th century. This was a job, he was not destined to last long in, his employment being swiftly terminated, after he lent his support to a union strike. He then went on to be briefly employed as a Carriage Driver, and eventually as a Gas Street Lamp Lighter. Exactly when and where he met his wife and married her is unclear, but what is known is they had their first child together, a daughter, in 1905, and had settled into a small terraced house at Albert Grove, Wavertree, by the time George's mother Louise French, their fourth child, was born in March 1911, appearing there with her on that year's census, taken a little under a month later.

John French.	Head.	35		Married	✓				Lamp-lighter.	409	Liverpool Corporation
Louise French.	Wife.		31	Married.	✓	4	4				
Kathleen Ellen French.	Daughter		6								
Mary Elizabeth French.	Daughter		3								
John French.	Son.	2									
Louise French.	Daughter.	under one month									

George Harrison's mother, recorded as a baby under one month old, with her siblings and parents at 11 Albert Grove, Wavetree, Liverpool, 1911 census. *Crown Copyright Class: RG14; Piece: 22669*

Louise's mother, Louise Woollam, George's maternal grandmother, was, like her husband, a newcomer to Liverpool, though she had been born not far away from the city in the picturesque village of Little Crosby, ten miles to the north, her father John Woollam, at the time in service there, as Head Gardener, to the Blundell family of Crosby Hall, for centuries one of the most powerful and influential Catholic families of Lancashire.

The gardens at Crosby Hall, Little Crosby, the care and cultivation of which was charged to George Harrison's great-grandfather, John Woollam (1837-90), a Professional Gardener, and son of another Professional Gardener, Roger Woollam (1810-58). George Harrison himself later became a keen and enthusiastic hobby gardener at his home in Oxfordshire.

The origins of the Woollam family lie even further afield, John himself originally born in St Martins, Shropshire, the son of another Professional Gardener, Roger Woollam, and grandson of Charles Woollam, who had at one time farmed a large plot of 127 acres at Ifton Rhyn, dwarfing the lands Louise's husband's ancestors the Ffrench family had been forced to subsist on at the very same time in Ireland. George's great-grandfather, John Woollam, had first been married, at the age of twenty-five, to Isabella Flannagan, an Irish woman, and together at Crosby Hall, they had two children, Margaret and John Woollam, junior, born to them. Isabella then sadly died, John being recorded as widowed, with his two children, occupying the Gardener's Lodge at Crosby Hall on the census of 1871. Also, in his household that year, no doubt employed to help with the small children, was a fourteen-year-old servant, Lydia Daniels. She was the daughter of James Daniels, a labourer at the nearby Alkali works in Farnworth and it is through her that the widower John met his second wife, Lydia's elder sister, George Harrison's great-grandmother, Jane Daniels, a Dressmaker, who despite ta thirteen-year age gap between them, was married to John in late autumn 1872.

[99]

They went on to have a further three children, the youngest of which, George's grandmother, Louise, was born in 1879. Sadly, John died when she was just eleven years of age, and a few years on, in order to support her widowed mother Jane, the teenage Louise travelled the short distance to Liverpool in search of work, finding employment once there as a Domestic Maid in local wealthy houses.

There is also, further back, through the Woollam family the suggestion of some Welsh ancestry for George Harrison, his great-great grandparents, Roger and Ann Woollam, being married in Wales in 1835, and the census records showing his great-great grandmother, Ann Woollam, *nee* Swallow, as a native of Dyffryn Aled in Llansannan, Denbighshire, Wales, where parish records confirm she was born in the spring of 1812.

George's great-grandfather John Woollam, aged fourteen, living in the Old Shop, St Martins, Shropshire, with his parents Roger and Ann Woollam, on the 1851 census, Ann's birthplace recorded as Denbighshire, Wales.
Crown Copyright Class: HO107; Piece: 1993; Folio: 723; Page: 21; GSU roll: 87394-87395

Technically this gives George the most rounded ancestry of all the Beatles, the only one with immediate ancestors born in every part of the British Isles, England, Scotland, Wales, Ireland and the Isle of Man. However, whilst undeniably accurate, this is slightly disingenuous, as despite her Welsh birth, both Ann Swallow's parents were in fact English born, her father John being born in Suffolk in 1778, and her mother Benedicta being born in Sussex in 1784. They had married in Wales in the opening years of the 19th century, having moved there in the course of John's trade as a Licensed Victualler, though he would eventually end his days there working as a Confectioner. Most of his children, Ann included, had crossed back over to England within a generation, several settling in and around Liverpool. It is true to say that whilst they all share plentiful Irish and English ancestry, of all the Beatles, only John Lennon can truly lay claim to any real native Welsh ancestry.

After their 1930 marriage, George Harrison's parents, Harold and Louise, settled into domestic life together at 12 Arnold Grove, Wavertree, Liverpool. Their first child, a daughter, like both her mother and grandmother named as Louise, was born in the August of 1931, with a son, Harry Harrison, named for his late grandfather, following on in 1934. Shortly after this Harold Harrison, tiring of life away from home and family, gave up the call of the sea altogether, and returned to dry land, finding regular work as a Liverpool Bus Conductor, later being promoted to a Driver.

A third child, son Peter, was born to the family after the outbreak of the Second World War in July 1940. He would go on to attend Dovedale Primary School, sharing classes with the young John Lennon, just a few months his junior. However, it was to be another war baby, the Harrison's fourth and final child, born to them there on the night of 24th February 1943, who would later forge a more enduring link with his elder brother's classmate, and find fame for himself, the end point of this particular ancestral trail, Beatle, George Harrison.

[100]

Ancestry of George Harrison

Edward Harrison

b: 13 Jan 1848 in Etna Street, Stanley, West...
m: 24 May 1868 in Liverpool, Lancashire,....
d: Jun 1925 in 12 Macqueen Street, Old Swan,...

Henry "Harry" Harrison

b: 21 Jan 1882 in 12 Queen Street, Old Swan,
West Derby, Liverpool, Lancashire, England
m: 17 Aug 1902 in Holy Trinity Wavertree,
Liverpool, Lancashire, England
d: 25 Sep 1915 in Battle of Loos, Haisnes, Pas
De Calais, France
Occupation: Master Bricklayer

Elizabeth Hargreaves

b: Nov 1850 in 9 Holgate Street, Manchester,
Lancashire, England

Harold Hargreaves Harrison

b: 28 May 1909 in Wavertree, Liverpool,
Lancashire, England
m: 20 May 1930 in Brownlow Hill Register Office,
Liverpool, Lancashire, England
d: 1978 in Warrington, Cheshire, England
Occupation: Ship Steward/Bus Conductor

James Davidson Thompson

b: 10 Apr 1857 in Kirkinner, Wigtownshire,....
m: 20 Nov 1878 in Liverpool Lancashire, England
d: Jan 1925 in 3 Wellington Grove, Wavertree,....

Jane Thompson

b: 1884 in Wellington Road, Wavertree, Liverpool,
Lancashire, England
Occupation: Confectioner's Assistant

Annie Caley

b: 1856 in Ramsey, Isle of Man
d: 1939 in Wavertree, Liverpool, Lancashire,
England

George Harrison

b: 24 Feb 1943 in 12 Arnold Grove, Liverpool,
Lancashire, England
Occupation: Musician, Guitarist, Song Writer,
Gardener

James Darby Ffrench

b: Camolin, County Wexford, Ireland (Circa 1839)
d: 1907 in Corah, Tombrack, County Wexford
Ireland

John French

b: 31 Mar 1870 in Ferns, County Wexford, Ireland
d: 1937 in Liverpool, Lancashire, England
Occupation: Agricultural
Labourer/Policeman/Carriage Driver/Lamp Lighter

Ellen Whelan

b: County Wexford, Ireland (Circa 1840)
d: 1906 in Corah, Tombrack, County Wexford,
Ireland

Louise French

b: 10 Mar 1911 in Wavertree, Liverpool,
Lancashire, England
d: 07 Jul 1970 in Warrington, Cheshire, England
Occupation: Shop Assistant

John Woollam

b: 1837 in St Martins, Shropshire, England
m: 25 Nov 1872 in St Mary's, Widnes, Lancashire,
England

Louisa Woollam

b: 1879 in Virgins Lane, Little Crosby, Sefton,
Lancashire, England
d: 1948 in Liverpool, Lancashire, England
Occupation: Domestic Maid

Jane Daniels

b: Nov 1850 in Farnworth, Widnes, Lancashire,
England
Occupation: Dressmaker

Ancestry of George Harrison's Paternal Grandfather Henry "Harry" Harrison

Anthony Harrison
b: 29 Apr 1797 in Eccleston, Prescot,....
m: 01 Dec 1816 in St James, Toxteth Park,....
d: 1863 in Deys Lane, West Derby, Liverpool....

Elizabeth Orrett
b: 1796 in West Derby, Liverpool, Lancashire....
d: West Derby, Liverpool, Lancashire, England....

Robert Shepherd
b: Lancashire, England (Circa 1795)
d: 28 Oct 1813 in St Peter's, Liverpool,....
d: 1846 in Prescot Road, Old Swan, West....

Mary Webster
b: 23 Jul 1788 in Ford, Sefton, Lancashire,....
d: West Derby, Liverpool, Lancashire, England....
Occupation: House Servant

James Hargreaves
b: 1793 in Haslingden, Lancashire, England
m: 06 Jul 1818 in Haslingden, Lancashire,....
d: 1872 in Manchester, Lancashire, England

Betty Hindle
b: 1797 in Haslingden, Lancashire, England
d: 1859 in Manchester, Lancashire, England

Samuel Holmes
b: 1791 in Manchester, Lancashire, England
m: 18 Dec 1815 in St John, Manchester,....
d: Manchester, Lancashire, England (Between....

Alice Adkin
b: (Circa 1786)
d: Manchester, Lancashire, England (After 1841)

Robert Harrison
b: 09 Oct 1816 in West Derby, Liverpool, Lancashire, England
m: 15 Nov 1835 in St Nicholas, Liverpool, Lancashire, England
d: Mar 1877 in Highfield Road, Old Swan, West Derby, Liverpool, Lancashire, England
Occupation: Joiner (Employing 1 man and 1 boy 1861)

Jane Shepherd
b: 1814 in Litherland, Sefton, Lancashire, England
d: Jul 1888 in 9 Springfield Street, Old Swan, West Derby, Liverpool, Lancashire, England

John Hargreaves
b: 1821 in Haslingden, Lancashire, England
m: 1842 in Skipton, Yorkshire, England
d: 1860 in Manchester, Lancashire, England
Occupation: Agricultural Labourer/Carter/Carrier

Ann Holmes
b: 1821 in Manchester, Lancashire, England
d: West Derby, Liverpool, Lancashire, England (After 1871)
Occupation: Silk Winder

Edward Harrison
b: 13 Jan 1848 in Etna Street, Stanley, West Derby, Liverpool, Lancashire, England
m: 24 May 1868 in Liverpool, Lancashire, England
d: Jun 1925 in 12 Macqueen Street, Old Swan, West Derby, Liverpool, Lancashire, England
Occupation: Stonemason

Elizabeth Hargreaves
b: Nov 1850 in 9 Holgate Street, Manchester, Lancashire, England
d: 1920 in 12 Macqueen Street, Old Swan, West Derby, Liverpool, Lancashire, England

Henry "Harry" Harrison
b: 21 Jan 1882 in 12 Queen Street, Old Swan, West Derby, Liverpool, Lancashire, England
m: 17 Aug 1902 in Holy Trinity Wavertree, Liverpool, Lancashire, England
d: 25 Sep 1915 in Battle of Loos, Halsnes, Pas De Calais, France
Occupation: Master Bricklayer

Ancestry of Robert Harrison

Robert Harrison
b: 09 Oct 1816 in West Derby, Liverpool, Lancashire, England
m: 15 Nov 1835 in St Nicholas, Liverpool, Lancashire, England
d: Mar 1877 in Highfield Road, Old Swan, West Derby, Liverpool, Lancashire, England
Occupation: Joiner (Employing 1 man and 1 boy 1861)

Anthony Harrison
b: 29 Apr 1797 in Eccleston, Prescot, Lancashire, England
m: 01 Dec 1816 in St James, Toxteth Park, Liverpool, Lancashire, England
d: 1863 in Deys Lane, West Derby, Liverpool, Lancashire, England
Occupation: Joiner

Elizabeth Orrett
b: 1796 in West Derby, Liverpool, Lancashire, England
d: West Derby, Liverpool, Lancashire, England (Between 1851-61)

Robert Harrison
m: 08 Sep 1794 in St Elphin, Warrington, Lancashire, England
Occupation: Farmer

Sarah Orrett
b: 1770 in Rainford, Lancashire, England

Ralph Orrett
b: 1768 in Rainford, Lancashire, England
m: 30 Aug 1794 in St James, Toxteth Park, Liverpool, Lancashire, England
Occupation: Farmer

Margaret Brownbill
b: 28 Jan 1770 in West Derby, Liverpool, Lancashire, England

Ralph Orrett
Occupation: Husbandman

Sarah

Ralph Orrett
Occupation: Husbandman

Sarah

Henry Brownbill
b: 1732 in West Derby, Liverpool, Lancashire, England

Margaret Stocker

[103]

Ancestry of George Harrison's Paternal Grandmother Jane Thompson

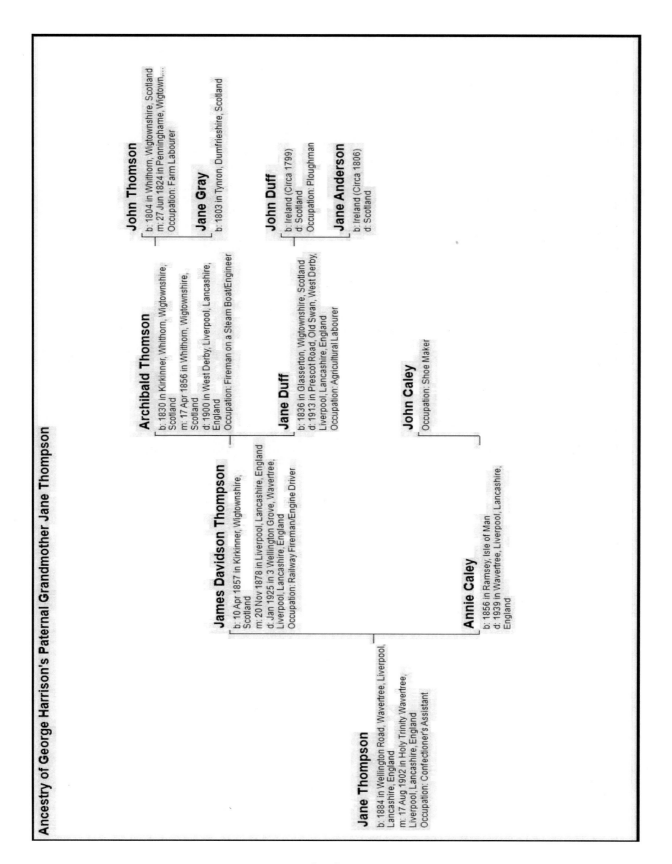

John Thomson
b: 1804 in Whithorn, Wigtownshire, Scotland
m: 27 Jun 1824 in Penninghame, Wigtown....
Occupation: Farm Labourer

Jane Gray
b: 1803 in Tynron, Dumfrieshire, Scotland

John Duff
b: Ireland (Circa 1799)
d: Scotland
Occupation: Ploughman

Jane Anderson
b: Ireland (Circa 1806)
d: Scotland

Archibald Thomson
b: 1830 in Kirkinner, Whithorn, Wigtownshire, Scotland
m: 17 Apr 1856 in Whithorn, Wigtownshire, Scotland
d: 1900 in West Derby, Liverpool, Lancashire, England
Occupation: Fireman on a Steam Boat/Engineer

Jane Duff
b: 1836 in Glasserton, Wigtownshire, Scotland
d: 1913 in Prescot Road, Old Swan, West Derby, Liverpool, Lancashire, England
Occupation: Agricultural Labourer

John Caley
Occupation: Shoe Maker

James Davidson Thompson
b: 10 Apr 1857 in Kirkinner, Wigtownshire, Scotland
m: 20 Nov 1878 in Liverpool, Lancashire, England
d: Jan 1925 in 3 Wellington Grove, Wavertree, Liverpool, Lancashire, England
Occupation: Railway Fireman/Engine Driver

Annie Caley
b: 1856 in Ramsey, Isle of Man
d: 1939 in Wavertree, Liverpool, Lancashire, England

Jane Thompson
b: 1884 in Wellington Road, Wavertree, Liverpool, Lancashire, England
m: 17 Aug 1902 in Holy Trinity Wavertree, Liverpool, Lancashire, England
Occupation: Confectioner's Assistant

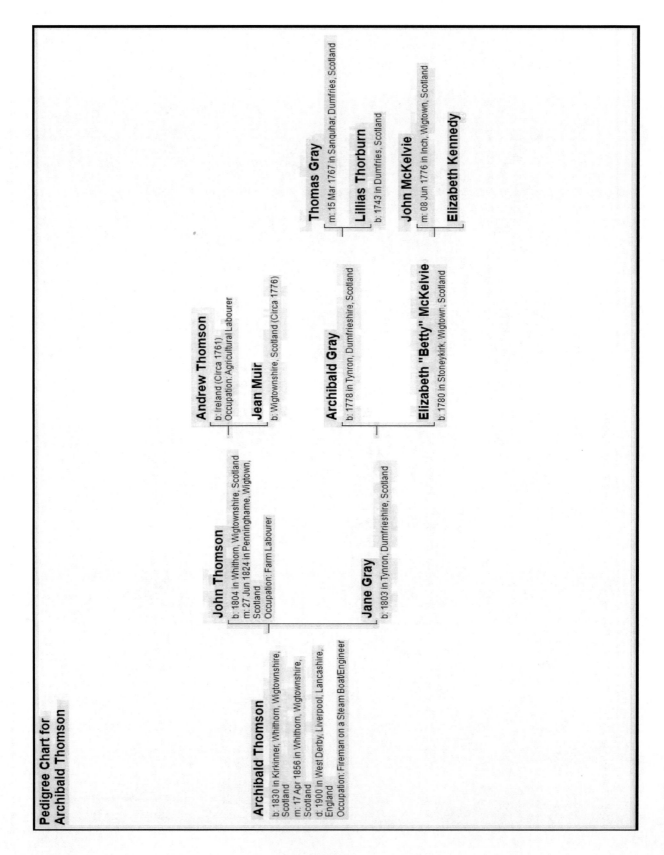

Archibald Thomson

b: 1830 in Kirkinner, Whithorn, Wigtownshire, Scotland
m: 17 Apr 1856 in Whithorn, Wigtownshire, Scotland
d: 1900 in West Derby, Liverpool, Lancashire, England
Occupation: Fireman on a Steam Boat/Engineer

John Thomson

b: 1804 in Whithorn, Wigtownshire, Scotland
m: 27 Jun 1824 in Penninghame, Wigtown, Scotland
Occupation: Farm Labourer

Jane Gray

b: 1803 in Tynron, Dumfrieshire, Scotland

Andrew Thomson

b: Ireland (Circa 1761)
Occupation: Agricultural Labourer

Jean Muir

b: Wigtownshire, Scotland (Circa 1776)

Archibald Gray

b: 1778 in Tynron, Dumfrieshire, Scotland

Elizabeth "Betty" McKelvie

b: 1780 in Stoneykirk, Wigtown, Scotland

Thomas Gray

m: 15 Mar 1767 in Sanquhar, Dumfries, Scotland

Lillias Thorburn

b: 1743 in Dumfries, Scotland

John McKelvie

m: 08 Jun 1776 in Inch, Wigtown, Scotland

Elizabeth Kennedy

Ancestry of George Harrison's Maternal Grandfather John French

John French

b: 31 Mar 1870 in Ferns, County Wexford, Ireland
d: 1937 in Liverpool, Lancashire, England

Occupation: Agricultural Labourer/Policeman/Carriage Driver/Lamp Lighter

James Darby Ffrench

b: Camolin, County Wexford, Ireland (Circa 1839)
d: 1907 in Corah, Tombrack, County Wexford, Ireland

Occupation: Agricultural Labourer

Ellen Whelan

b: County Wexford, Ireland (Circa 1840)
d: 1906 in Corah, Tombrack, County Wexford, Ireland

Ancestry of George Harrison's Maternal Grandmother Louisa Woollam

Charles Woollam

b: 1778 in Whixall, Shropshire, England
m: 07 Jul 1806 in St Martins, Shropshire, England
d: ifton Rhyn, St Martins, Shropshire, England....

Elizabeth Jones

b: 1790 in St Martins, Shropshire, England

Roger Woollam

b: 13 Jan 1810 in Ifton Rhyn, St Martins,
Shropshire, England
m: 30 May 1835 in Denbigh, Denbighshire, Wales
d: 1858 in Oswestry, Shropshire, England
Occupation: Gardener

John Swallow

b: 1778 in Stoke by Clare, Suffolk, England
m: 21 Apr 1806 in Caerwys, Flintshire, Wales
d: May 1854 in Llansannan, Denbighshire, Wales

Benedicta Edwards

b: 1784 in St Clements, Hastings, Sussex,.....
d: Nov 1815 in Dyffryn Aled, Llansannan.....

Ann Swallow

b: 13 Mar 1812 in Dyffryn Aled, Llansannan,
Denbighshire, Wales
Occupation: Housekeeper

John Woollam

b: 1837 in St Martins, Shropshire, England
m: 25 Nov 1872 in St Mary's, Widnes, Lancashire,
England
d: Nov 1890 in Little Crosby, Lancashire, England
Occupation: Farmer's Servant

James Daniels

b: (Circa 1790)
m: 27 Dec 1819 in All Saints, Rainford, St...
Occupation: Watch Maker

Elizabeth Fillingham

b: 06 Oct 1794 in St Helens, Prescot, Lancashire,
England

James Daniels

b: 1821 in Sutton, Prescot, Lancashire, England
m: 28 Jun 1846 in Our Lady and Saint Nicholas,
Liverpool, Lancashire, England
d: 1876 in Farnworth, Widnes, Lancashire,
England
Occupation: Carter/Chemical Labourer at an
Alkali Works

Thomas Roughsedge

b: 27 Jan 1791 in Rainhill, Prescot, Lancashire,.....
m: 10 Feb 1813 in St John's, Old Haymarket,.....
d: Rainhill, Prescot, Lancashire, England.....

Lydia Rimmer

b: 1790 in Sutton, Prescot, Lancashire, England
d: 1850 in Rainhill, Prescot, Lancashire, England

Mary Ann Roughsedge

b: 1824 in Rainhill, Prescot, Lancashire, England

Jane Daniels

b: Nov 1850 in Farnworth, Widnes, Lancashire,
England
Occupation: Dressmaker

Louisa Woollam

b: 1879 in Virgins Lane, Little Crosby, Sefton,
Lancashire, England
d: 1948 in Liverpool, Lancashire, England
Occupation: Domestic Maid

Ringo Starr

Like fellow Beatle George, Ringo Starr's ancestry in Liverpool can be traced back to the early days of the city's development as a commercial port, with at least one branch of his paternal ancestors, the Brownswords, on record there as early as the 1750s, and several others Ottys, Bowers, Henry and Steele all building their homes and plying trades as varied as Butter Merchant, Watch Tool Maker and White Smith, within the city confines, before the turn of the 19th century.

Born Richard Starkey in 9 Madyrn Street, Toxteth, Liverpool, on 7th July 1940, had it not been for a quirk of fate Ringo's surname might just have easily have been Parkin. His paternal grandfather John George Parkin, a Liverpool Boiler Maker, assumed the surname Starkey at the age of six, on his widowed mother's remarriage to Richard Starkey, a Soldier from Birkenhead.

George Henry Parkin, John's natural father, was an Iron Driller at the Mersey Ship Yards, and had passed away a year before this, in the early winter of 1891, at the age of twenty-six, at the Parkin family home in Tranmere, Cheshire. He had contracted the lung disease pleurisy after catching cold, a condition that, coincidentally, his great-grandson Ringo would also be struck down with as a thirteen-year-old schoolboy, spending near to two years in a sanatorium, narrowly cheating death, and never returning to his schooling afterward.

The Parkin family were not native Scousers, but had originally come to the Merseyside area in the 1850s when Ringo's 3 x great-grandfather, Samuel Parkin, a Yorkshire born blacksmith, moved there with his second wife, Welsh woman Mary Challender. Samuel's oldest son, Ringo's great-great grandfather, Samuel Parkin, junior, the only child to his first marriage, was married not long afterward, in the autumn of 1864 at St Nicholas's Church, Liverpool.

The bride of Samuel Parkin, junior, Mary Jane Preston, was, like her husband, also a native of Yorkshire by birth, but ultimately her family roots lay further afield, her father Richard Preston, a Merchant Navy man, and later Shipwright, having moved with his family from Durham in North East England, to Yorkshire, and then later again to Liverpool, in order to find work for himself on the ships in dock there.

[108]

A Shipwright at work. Ringo's 3 x great-grandfather Richard Preston, a Durham Shipwright, bought both his skills and his family to Liverpool in the mid-19th century.

In previous examinations on the Beatles ancestry it has often been claimed Ringo Starr is the only one of the four Beatles without Irish ancestry, something stated as fact by several of his biographers. A proper examination of his ancestry shows this is anything but the case. Liverpool has long and strong links with Ireland, being the first port of call for so many leaving that land. The 1841 census shows that almost one in five Liverpool inhabitants recorded Ireland as their birthplace, a figure which jumped to more than one in four by the time of the next census in 1851, doubtless as a result of the mass movement of displaced persons caused by the terrible years of famine in Ireland during the intervening ten years.

Therefore, Liverpool inhabitants without any Irish ancestry are few and far between, perhaps the exception rather than the rule. This is especially true for those with roots which stretch as far back in the city as Ringo's, and sure enough he can in fact claim three of his four great-grandmothers, one on his father side, and both on his mother's side, as either Irish born, or Liverpool born to Irish parents.

Irish emigrants in Victorian Liverpool. As in other parts of England and Scotland, the Irish often lived in the worse overcrowded inner-city slums, conditions nevertheless preferable to starvation in their homeland.

The first of these Irish links comes through the same ancestor from whom he ultimately acquired the Starkey surname, paternal great-grandmother Mary Elizabeth James. Born in Liverpool on the 13th August 1867, and baptised at St Nicholas Roman Catholic Church in the city, a little over two weeks later, Mary, or 'Polly' as she preferred to be known, was the last but one of seven children to her parents, and their only daughter. She married Ringo's great-grandfather, George Parkin, eldest son of Samuel Parkin and Mary Preston, in Everton, on 8th March 1886, at the age of eighteen.

Her father was Thaddeus John Edward James, a Journeyman Baker by trade, who had been bought to England from Ireland as a teenager, at the height of the Great Famine, by his own father John James, a Joiner, though where exactly the family departed from is not known.

Once in Liverpool, he married Sara Jane Steele, in 1857, at St Peter's Church, Everton. Twenty-three-year-old Sara was very much a local girl, born in the city, her father Francis Steel, a Sail Maker for the local ships, her mother, Mary Henry, the daughter of a Liverpool Butter Merchant. However, at least part of her family roots also originated in Ireland, her grandfather Francis Steel, senior, having moved from Ireland to Liverpool as a young man in the closing years of the 18th century, marrying into another, by then well established, local Liverpool family, the Brownswords.

Through this great-grandmother then, 'Polly' James/Parkin/Starkey, who died nine years before his birth, Ringo not only gets his first drop of Irish blood from her father, but his deepest Scouse roots from her mother. Having originally moved from Liverpool to nearby Tranmere, where Ringo's grandfather was born, after her second marriage to Richard Starkey, Polly moved again, first to Ruabon in Wales, where a daughter was born to her, and then back again to Tranmere where she had two more daughters. Eventually however, Richard and Polly Starkey made the fateful decision to move back to her city of birth Liverpool, renting a house at 46 Star Street, Toxteth, around the turn of the 20th century. Here another five children would be born into the Starkey family, and here they would remain thereafter.

Ringo's great-grandmother Polly Starkey/James, with her family at 52 Star Street, Toxteth on the census of April 1901. Ringo's grandfather John Starkey/Parkin is recorded as a fourteen-year-old steel rivet handler.
Crown Copyright, Class: RG13; Piece: 3428; Folio: 143; Page: 45

On the 31st July 1910, at their local parish church St Matthews, Toxteth, Polly's eldest son, John Starkey, Ringo's grandfather, was married, at the age of twenty three, to the twenty-year-old Annie Bower.

Annie, Ringo's paternal grandmother, through her father's Bower family, provide him with family links in Liverpool almost as long standing as his grandfather's. Their roots can be traced at least as far back as John Bower and Elizabeth Briske, Annie's great-great grandparents, who were married in St George's Church, Liverpool, in the year 1766.

Their son, John Bower, Annie's great-grandfather, became a successful Stonemason in the city, building many local houses and buildings, including his own home in Toxteth's Grafton Street, where both Annie's grandfather David and father Alfred Bower were later born, and just a stone's throw or two away from where Ringo himself would later be born.
Annie's grandfather, David Bower, however, did not follow his own father into the Stonemason's trade, instead becoming a Joiner, though both the wealth he inherited from his father's endeavours, and the property portfolio, allowed him to describe himself as a 'Proprietor of Houses' and a 'Gentleman' on the various surviving census and parish record documents. His wife Amy Teale, Ringo's great-great

[110]

grandmother, was also the daughter of a successful Liverpool Stonemason, Thomas Teale. Thomas is the second Yorkshireman in Ringo's tree, being born there around the year 1795. Before moving for his trade to Liverpool, Thomas first set up business in Scotland, where he had met and married his wife, Marion Foggo, in Edinburgh, in October 1819.

Thomas and Marion Teal[e], Ringo's 3 x great-grandparents,
178 Great Howard Street, Liverpool, 1851 Census.
Crown Copyright, Class: HO107; Piece: 2177; Folio: 859; Page: 18; GSU roll: 87172-87174

Edinburgh, Scotland, painted by J.M.W Turner (1775-1851), in 1819, the same year Ringo's 3 x great-grandparents, Scotswoman Marion Foggo and Yorkshireman Thomas Teale, were married there.
The National Gallery of Scotland

From Marion, his 3-x great-grandmother, Ringo gets his first drop of Scottish blood, though like his Irish links, much more would be inherited through his mother's side. This remarkable woman was widowed in Liverpool at just forty-nine years of age, but rather than search around for re-marriage, like so many women of her time, with the proceeds of her late husband's estate she instead set herself up in business independently, running the "*Dumfries and Galloway Inn and Public House*" in the city, an obvious affectionate nod to her own Scottish birth and heritage.

18**41**. Marriage solemnized *at S¹ Phillip Church* in the *Parish* of *Liverpool* in the County of *Lancaster*

No.	When Married.	Name and Surname.	Age.	Condition.	Rank or Profession.	Residence at the Time of Marriage.	Father's Name and Surname.	Rank or Profession of Father.
408	*March 23ᵈ*	*David Bower*	*full age*	*Bachelor*	*Joiner*	*Bercom Street*	*John Bower*	*Dead*
		Amey Teal	*17 years*	*Spinster*	—	*Hunter Street*	*Thomas Teal*	*Stone mason*

Married in the *Church Of S¹ Phillip* according to the Rites and Ceremonies of the *Established church* *by me, B¹ ——* *9 T. Bant*

This Marriage was solemnized between us, *David Bower* *Amey Teal*

in the Presence of us, *Richard Roberts* *Sarah Bower*

1841 Marriage of Ringo's great-great grandparents, David Bower and Amy Teal(e), daughter of Thomas Teale and Marion Foggo, at St Phillip's Church, Liverpool. *Liverpool Record Office reference number: 283 PLP/3/7*

Ringo's great-grandfather Alfred Bower, David Bower and Amy Teale's son, became the second generation to decline to follow in his own father's footsteps, rather than become a Joiner, instead entering into the trade of a Tinsmith. He was married to Margaret Ellen Parr, on 10ᵗʰ November 1873 in Toxteth. Her father Joseph Parr was also a Tinsmith, sometime Coppersmith, and doubtless this business link is how the two families originally met.

Tinsmith at work, around the same time, 1900, as Ringo Starr's ancestors followed the trade.

[112]

Unlike the Bower family, the Parrs were not native to Liverpool, Joseph having been originally born in Cheshire, before moving to Oswestry, Shropshire where he met and married his wife, the couple moving again together twelve years after their marriage to Liverpool, where Margaret, the youngest of their nine children would be born in the spring of 1854.

Ringo's father, Richard Henry Parkin Starkey, named for both step-grandfather Richard Starkey, and great-uncle Henry Parkin, was born on 1st October 1913, a little more than three years on from the marriage of his parents, John and Annie Starkey, the second of their four children. Whilst he was still under a year old the First World War broke out, and his father John Starkey, then aged twenty-eight, joined up to fight as a Private in the Liverpool Regiment. He would be away from his home for the next six years, remaining in Cologne, Germany, as part of the British Occupation Force, after the end of the war, and would not see his two sons again until they were nine and seven respectively.

Men from the King's Liverpool Regiment, taken on their way to the Front in France WWI.

With her husband away, Ringo's grandmother Annie no doubt relied on help from her mother-in-law, Polly Starkey, who lived in a house just two doors away from her in Vere Street, Toxteth, with her younger unmarried daughters and sons. However, tragedy would hit the Starkey family during these war years, when in the closing months of the conflict, the worst pandemic of the century, the Spanish Influenza spread across the globe, attacking the young and healthy, infecting one third of humanity, and leaving over thirty million dead in its wake. To put this appalling toll into full context, this amounted to five times as many casualties in a single year as had been created by the four years of bloody and mechanised slaughter in France at the same time.

Among the many poor unfortunate victims of this dreadful scourge was Ringo's great-aunt Mary Parkin Starkey who also lived on Vere Street, and died twenty-eight days before the Armistice ending the war was signed. The only full sister to Ringo's grandfather, John Starkey, born to Polly Starkey's first marriage to George Parkin, she was just twenty-nine years of age at the time of her death and left behind four young children and a husband.

 How the death of this young auntie affected Ringo's father, occurring just two weeks after his fifth birthday, we can't know, though with his father away too it must clearly have been a very sad time for the family indeed. On the eventual return home of John Starkey, two more children were born into the family, a pair of sisters for Richard and elder brother John, Annie and May Starkey, born in 1922 and 1927 respectively. By the time of May's birth, the fifteen-year-old Richard Starkey had left his schooling and found employment as a Confectioner in a local bakery. It was here he would meet the girl he would later marry, when he was twenty-two and she twenty-one, Ringo Starr's mother, Elsie Gleave.

[113]

Ringo's great-aunt, Mary Parkin/Starkey/Brown, (1889-1918), sister to Ringo's grandfather John. A victim aged 29 to one of the worst global pandemics in modern history.
Photo Courtesy of Janet Tranter

Ringo's mother Elsie Gleave/Starkey (right), and his aunt Annie *'Nancy'* Starkey, taken in the mid-1960s.
Photo courtesy of Janet Tranter

Elsie's family the Gleaves were originally from Warrington, Lancashire. Ringo's 3 x great-grandfather Peter Gleave, a Wire Worker and Boiler Maker, can be found, aged sixty-five, on the 1871 census, as an inmate of the Warrington Workhouse. He died a six years later.

These reduced circumstances may have been what motivated his son William Gleave, Ringo's great-great grandfather, to come to Liverpool, where he was married in summer 1863, at St Bride's Church, to twenty-nine-year-old Toxteth girl, Mary Openshaw. The marriage records William's occupation, like father Peter's, as a Boiler Maker, and wife Mary was recorded as the daughter of a Liverpool Cow Keeper and Dairyman, Thomas Openshaw.

Like the Starkey family, the Gleaves settled down into married life in the Toxteth region of Liverpool, not far from the location of the Openshaw family home. William and Mary Gleave's first son, William Gleave, junior, Ringo's great-grandfather, was born in 1867, one of eight children born to his parents' marriage. From his early teen years, he followed his father and grandfather into the trade of Boiler Maker, and was married shortly after his twenty-second birthday, in the summer of 1889, at St Michael's, Toxteth Park, to the nineteen-year-old Mary Catherine Conroy. Mary Kate, as she preferred to be known, is the great-grandmother who provides Ringo with his second link to Ireland.

Baptised, at two weeks of age, on 21st November 1869, at St Anthony's Roman Catholic Church, Scotland Road, the same chapel so important to the Irish community in Liverpool, also frequented by both Paul McCartney and John Lennon's ancestors, her parents were William Conroy, a Painter and Engine Driver, and Dublin born Maria Jane O'Connor. They had been married a year before on 23rd October 1868 in another of the city's Catholic chapels, St Mary's, recording their respective parents as Patrick Conroy and Thomas O'Connor.

Baptism of Ringo Starr's great-grandmother, Mary Catherine Conroy, 7th November 1869, at St Anthony's Roman Catholic Church, Liverpool. *Liverpool Record Office Reference Number: 282 ANT/1/9*

So far, no trace has been found of William Conroy or Maria Jane O'Connor in Liverpool before their marriage, so it is possible they had both come over from Ireland not long before this date. Certainly, their daughter Mary Kate was proud of her Irish roots, despite being born in England herself, later recording Irish for her nationality on the census of 1911.

The Gleaves, 3 Loxdale Street, Toxteth, April 1911. Ringo's great-grandmother, Mary Kate Conroy/Gleave, recording her nationality as Irish. *Crown Copyright Class: RG14; Piece: 22246*

[115]

After their marriage, Mary Kate and her husband William Gleave had seven children together, all baptised in the father's religious and cultural tradition, rather than the mother's, as Protestants.

The second child, Ringo Starr's maternal grandfather, John Gleave, was born on 11th April 1891, at 11 Moville Street, Toxteth Park, Liverpool. Originally, he followed into the family trade, becoming the fourth generation of Gleaves to work as a Boiler Maker. Later, however, he found alternative employment in the local tin works, before, like Ringo's paternal grandfather John Starkey, volunteering for Military Service at the outbreak of the First World War, in his case being assigned to the 9th Battalion Royal Lancashire Artillery, where he eventually attained the rank of Bombardier.

A fine example of the tough breed of men that were the Boiler Makers. Both Ringo's grandfathers followed this trade, his mother's family the Gleaves providing four successive generation of Liverpool Boiler Makers. Their boilers were destined to power the engine rooms of the many ships coming in and out of the great port.

Photo by Waldemar Titzenthaler, circa 1900, Harvard University

Four months before this he had been married in Liverpool, on 12th April 1914, to Catherine Martha Johnson, Ringo's mother Elsie being the first child born to them at the family home Toxteth, six months on, and just two months after the outbreak of the war which would subsequently see her father absent from the family home for much of her first formative years.

At the time of their marriage in 1914, Ringo's grandparents were both twenty-two, the couple having been born barely a fortnight apart from each other in the April of 1891. Ringo's grandmother Catherine Johnson, or '*Kitty*' as she was known to her family, was, like her husband, also from Irish stock, providing Ringo with his third and final link to the land.

The census records reveal, her mother, Mary Elizabeth Cunningham, known as '*Minnie*', was born around the year 1852, in Rostrevor, County Down, a small village, in the shadow of the Mourne mountains, just outside of Newry, where band mates John Lennon and Paul McCartney's family roots also originate, the third Beatle link to this area of modern day Northern Ireland.

Twenty-four years old at the time of her marriage, in Liverpool, in April 1875, when exactly Minnie came to England from Ireland is unknown, and her movements before cannot yet be traced with any certainty.

No.	When Married.	Name and Surname.	Age.	Condition.	Rank or Profession.	Residence at the time of Marriage.	Father's Name and Surname.	Rank or Profession of Father.
495	April 14 1875	Andrew Johnson	full	Bachelor	Mariner	Liverpool	Peter Johnson	Mariner
		Mary Elizabeth Cunningham	full	Spinster	—	Liverpool	James Cunningham	Gardener

Marriage of Mary Elizabeth '*Minnie*' Cunningham and Andrew Johnson, Ringo Starr's great-grandparents, St Thomas, Liverpool, April 14th 1875. *Liverpool Record Office Reference Number: 283 THO/3/7*

On her wedding document she recorded her father as James Cunningham, a Gardener. Her mother Elizabeth appears as widowed, living in her daughter's household, on every census record in England, so both may have travelled over to Liverpool together shortly after the death of James, to find work to support themselves, which was always more plentiful for single women in cities such as Liverpool, then in small towns and villages, especially in Ireland, still struggling to recover from the devastating and depopulating effects of the famine two decades previous.

Intriguingly, though Minnie's mother, Elizabeth, Ringo's great-great grandmother, also records County Down, Ireland as her birth place on the four censuses she appears on 1871-1901, she instead recorded it as Faversham, Kent, in England, on the final census where she appears, in 1911, at the grand age of ninety-two. This raises the possibility, despite Minnie's own birth in Northern Ireland, the Cunningham family may have originally been English settlers to that land as well.

Minnie's husband, Ringo's great-grandfather, was also a newcomer to both Liverpool and England, originally hailing from north of the border in Scotland. First appearing in Liverpool on the 1871 census, Andrew Johnson, then a nineteen-year-old Seaman, was recorded lodging with his younger sister Ursula Johnson, in a household with several other Scottish sailors of varying ages.

Andrew's roots ultimately lay in the most far flung northern limit of the British Isles, the Shetlands, where he was born in May 1824 to Peter Johnson, also a Sailor and Fisherman, and his wife Phillis *'Philadelphia'* Tait, who span worsted and farmed their small hold four acres of land while her husband was away at sea.

South Voxter, Delting, Shetlands Islands, birthplace of Ringo's great-grandfather Andrew Johnson, a Fisherman who later married and settled in Liverpool with his wife, Irish born Mary *'Minnie'* Cunningham
Photo Mike Pennington

Kirstie Anderson *nee* Robertson, and daughter Teena, carding and spinning wool, at the Pund of Voe, Delting, Shetlands, circa 1911. Ringo Starr's great-great grandmother, Janet Tait, *nee* Robertson, very possibly a relative of Kirstie, was recorded in the very same house, following the same occupation, half a century earlier in 1861
Photo Shetland Museum and Archives Photo Library

Shetland Islander's play tennis circa 1889. The house beyond the hill is the Pund at Voe, where Ringo Starr's Tait ancestors lived from at least 1841-62.
Photo Shetland Museum and Archives Photo Library

Despite these apparent Scottish roots, which he shares with only one other Beatle George Harrison, and like his Irish ancestry, he can claim on both mother and father's side, Ringo's Shetland ancestors were in fact far more likely to have originally been of Viking rather than Celtic stock. The Shetland Islands were in a peculiar position in the British Isles, for hundreds of years part of Norway rather than Scotland, a dialect of Norse still spoken amongst inhabitants to this day. Andrew Johnson's grandfather, Ringo's 3 x great-grandfather, is recorded in the parish records as Magnus Johnson, a farmer in Delting.

The Scandinavian overtones are clear enough, but an examination of his father John Johnson, a Fisherman, and the wider Johnson family, in the 18th century, Delting parish registers seems to banish any doubt with the family frequently not recording their surname as 'Johnson', as might be expected, but instead sons are recorded as '*Laurenceson*' or '*Peterson*' and daughters as '*Jamesdaughter*' '*Arthursdaughter*' a clear indication this family, rather than follow British customs, were until fairly recent times, following Scandinavian naming traditions, directly traceable back to their Norwegian and, ultimately, Viking forebears.

[118]

Though a seafaring man, Andrew Johnson eventually settled down with his new wife in Liverpool, remaining there until his death, in the family home at Toxteth, in 1927, at the age of seventy-five. His granddaughter Elsie, Ringo's mother, was at this time thirteen, so sadly he would not live to see her marry, or the child, born to her a decade or so on, in Toxteth, whose musical legacy, as an integral part of the greatest pop group of the twentieth century, would spread across the world, beating a trail extending out further still than the long and varied paths travelled by his colourful array of ancestors, not least of whom Andrew, who trod the path before him.

Ringo's great-grandfather, Shetlander, Andrew Johnson, recorded as a *'dock bound'* Seaman, with his family, including Ringo's grandmother Catherine, nineteen, great-grandmother Mary Kate, fifty-nine, and great-great grandmother, Elizabeth Cunningham, ninety-two, at 18 Tavistock Street, Dingle, Toxteth, Liverpool 1911.
Crown Copyright Class: RG14; Piece: 22234

***Up Helly Aa* festival, the annual Shetlands celebration of Viking roots**

Ancestry of Ringo Starr

George Henry Parkin

b: 1865 in Birkenhead, Cheshire, England
m: 08 Mar 1886 in St Peter's, Walton on the...
d: 07 Oct 1891 in 26 Princes Place, Tranmere,...

Mary Elizabeth "Polly" James

b: 13 Aug 1867 in Prince Edwin Lane, Everton, Liverpool, Lancashire, England

John George Parkin (Starkey)

b: 1886 in Tranmere, Birkenhead, Cheshire, England
m: 31 Jul 1910 in St Matthew's, Toxteth, Liverpool, Lancashire, England
d: 03 Oct 1959 in Sefton General Hospital, Liverpool, Lancashire, England
Occupation: Boiler Maker

Alfred Bower

b: May 1850 in 117 Grafton Street, Toxteth...
m: 10 Nov 1873 in St Michael's, Toxteth,...
d: Dec 1904 in 83 Northumberland Street,...

Margaret Ellen Parr

b: 1854 in Toxteth Park, Liverpool, Lancashire, England

Annie Bower

b: 22 Dec 1889 in 14 Goring Street, Toxteth, Liverpool, Lancashire, England
d: 07 Feb 1962 in The Homeopathic Hospital, Liverpool, Lancashire, England

Richard Henry Parkin Starkey

b: 01 Oct 1913 in 68 Toxteth Street, Liverpool, Lancashire, England
m: 24 Oct 1936 in St Silas, Toxteth, Liverpool, Lancashire, England
d: 1981 in Crewe, Cheshire, England
Occupation: Confectioner

William Gleave

b: 19 Mar 1867 in Toxteth, Liverpool, England
m: 10 Jun 1889 in St Michael's, Toxteth, Liverpool, England

Mary Catherine (Kate) Conroy

b: 07 Nov 1869 in Liverpool, England
d: 1916 in Toxteth, Liverpool, England

John Gleave

b: 11 Apr 1891 in 11 Moville Street, Toxteth, Liverpool, Lancashire, England
m: 12 Apr 1914 in St Matthews, Toxteth, Liverpool, England
d: 1936 in Toxteth, Liverpool, Lancashire, England
Occupation: Boiler Maker/Tin Works Labourer

Andrew Johnson

b: 02 Jan 1852 in Delting, Shetland, Scotland
m: 14 Apr 1875 in St Thomas, Toxteth,...
d: Sep 1927 in 18 Tavistock Steet, Toxteth,...

Mary Elizabeth "Minnie" Cunningham

b: Rostrevor, County Down, Ireland (Circa 1851)

Catherine Martha 'Kitty' Johnson

b: 28 Apr 1891 in 34 Gaskill Street, Toxteth, Liverpool, Lancashire, England
d: 1966 in Toxteth, Liverpool, Lancashire, England

Elsie Gleave

b: 19 Oct 1914 in 4 Hurrey Street, Toxteth, Liverpool, Lancashire, England
d: 1987 in Liverpool, Lancashire, England

Richard Starkey

b: 07 Jul 1940 in 9 Madryn Street, Liverpool, Lancashire, England
Occupation: Musician, Drummer, Singer, Actor

Ancestry of Ringo Starr's Paternal Grandfather John George Parkin (Starkey)

Samuel Parkin
b: 1805 in Birdwell, Leeds, Yorkshire, England
m: 14 Dec 1862 in St Nicholas, Liverpool,....
d: 1878 in Birkenhead, Cheshire, England

Samuel Parkin
b: 1838 in Sheffield, Yorkshire, England
m: 05 Sep 1864 in St Nicholas, Liverpool, England
d: 1892 in Birkenhead, Cheshire, England
Occupation: Blacksmith

Richard Preston
b: 07 Apr 1819 in Durham City, Durham, England
m: 08 Apr 1838 in St Thomas's Church....
Occupation: Merchant Navy Seaman/Shipwright

Mary Jane Preston
b: 1844 in Middlesborough, Yorkshire, England
d: 1881 in Birkenhead, Cheshire, England

Jane Black
b: Stockton On Tees, Durham, England (Circa 1816)
d: 1860 in Birkenhead, Cheshire, England

George Henry Parkin
b: 1865 in Birkenhead, Cheshire, England
m: 08 Mar 1886 in St Peter's, Walton on the Hill, Everton, Liverpool, Lancashire, England
d: 07 Oct 1891 in 26 Princes Place, Tranmere, Birkenhead, Cheshire, England
Occupation: Journeyman Iron Driller at a Ship Yard

John James
Occupation: Joiner

Thaddeus John Edward James
b: Ireland (Circa 1833)
m: 22 Feb 1857 in St Peter's, Walton on the Hill, Everton, Liverpool, Lancashire, England
d: 1898 in Birkenhead, Lancashire, England
Occupation: Baker

Francis Steele
b: 1814 in School Lane, Liverpool, Lancashire,....
m: 23 Feb 1835 in St Peter's, Walton on the....
d: 1888 in Everton, Liverpool, Lancashire,....

Sarah Jane Steele
b: 1835 in Everton, Liverpool, Lancashire, England
d: Oct 1869 in Prince Edwin Lane, Everton, Liverpool, Lancashire, England

Mary Henry
b: 19 Jul 1818 in Liverpool, Lancashire, England
d: 1873 in Everton, Liverpool, Lancashire, England

Mary Elizabeth "Polly" James
b: 13 Aug 1867 in Prince Edwin Lane, Everton, Liverpool, Lancashire, England
d: 1931 in Toxteth, Liverpool, Lancashire, England

John George Parkin (Starkey)
b: 1886 in Tranmere, Birkenhead, Cheshire, England
m: 31 Jul 1910 in St Matthew's, Toxteth, Liverpool, Lancashire, England
d: 03 Oct 1959 in Sefton General Hospital, Liverpool, Lancashire, England
Occupation: Boiler Maker

[121]

Pedigree Chart for Sarah Jane Steele

Francis Steele
b: Ireland (Circa 1770)
m: 31 Oct 1803 in St Thomas, Toxteth, Liverpool, England
d: 1849 in Liverpool, Lancashire, England
Occupation: Whitesmith/Porter

Thomas Brownsword
b: 06 Oct 1756 in Liverpool, Lancashire, England
m: 11 Jun 1780 in Walton on the Hill, Liverpool,....
d: Feb 1788 in Renshaw Street, Liverpool,....

Catherine "Kitty" Brownsword
b: 22 Nov 1784 in Liverpool, Lancashire, England
d: 1854 in Liverpool, Lancashire, England

Mary Garnet

Francis Steele
b: 1814 in School Lane, Liverpool, Lancashire, England
m: 23 Feb 1835 in St Peter's, Walton on the Hill, Everton, Liverpool, Lancashire, England
d: 1888 in Everton, Liverpool, Lancashire, England
Occupation: Sail Maker

Daniel Henry
m: 07 Apr 1803 in Holy Trinity, Liverpool, Lancashire, England
Occupation: Butter Merchant

Elizabeth Matthews

Mary Henry
b: 19 Jul 1818 in Liverpool, Lancashire, England
d: 1873 in Everton, Liverpool, Lancashire, England

Sarah Jane Steele
b: 1835 in Everton, Liverpool, Lancashire, England
m: 22 Feb 1857 in St Peter's, Walton on the Hill, Everton, Liverpool, Lancashire, England
d: Oct 1869 in Prince Edwin Lane, Everton, Liverpool, Lancashire, England

[122]

Ancestry of Ringo Starr's Paternal Grandmother Annie Bower

John Bower
b: 1778 in Liverpool, Lancashire, England
m: 06 Feb 1803 in Richmond St Anne....
d: 03 Jan 1823 in Grafton Street, Toxteth Park,...

Jane Otty
b: 24 Apr 1772 in Dale Street, Liverpool,....
d: Jul 1831 in Grafton Street, Toxteth Park,...

Thomas Teale
b: Yorkshire, England (Circa 1795)
m: 11 Oct 1819 in Edinburgh, Midlothian,....
d: 1851 in Liverpool, Lancaster, England

Marion Foggo
b: Loanhead, Edinburgh, Scotland (Circa 1801)
d: 1866 in Liverpool, Lancaster, England
Occupation: Victualler"Dumfries & Galloway....

Joseph Parr
b: 1787 in Neston, Cheshire, England
Occupation: Brazier

Jane
b: (Circa1790)

David Bower
b: 1818 in Grafton Street, Toxteth Park, Liverpool,
Lancashire, England
m: 23 Mar 1841 in St Philips, Toxteth, Liverpool,
Lancashire, England
d: 03 Mar 1890 in 11 Munrow Street, Toxteth
Park, Liverpool, Lancashire, England
Occupation: Joiner/Proprietor of Houses

Amy Teale
b: 18 Dec 1823 in Skipton in Craven, Yorkshire,
England
d: 31 Mar 1888 in Toxteth Park, Liverpool,
Lancashire, England

Joseph Parr
b: 1810 in Neston, Cheshire, England
m: 28 May 1832 in Oswestry, Shropshire,
England
d: Apr 1881 in 196 Mann Street, Toxteth Park,
Liverpool, Lancashire, England
Occupation: Tinsmith

Catherine Rodenhurst
b: 1812 in Oswestry, Shropshire, England
d: Jun 1871 in Star Street, Toxteth Park,
Liverpool, Lancashire, England

Alfred Bower
b: May 1850 in 117 Grafton Street, Toxteth Park,
Liverpool, Lancashire, England
m: 10 Nov 1873 in St Michael's, Toxteth,
Liverpool, England
d: Dec 1904 in 83 Northumberland Street, Toxteth
Park, Liverpool, Lancashire, England
Occupation: Tinsmith/Sheet Iron Worker

Margaret Ellen Parr
b: 1854 in Toxteth Park, Liverpool, Lancashire,
England
d: Jul 1918 in 58 Hughson Street, Toxteth Park,
Liverpool, England

Annie Bower
b: 22 Dec 1889 in 14 Goring Street, Toxteth,
Liverpool, Lancashire, England
m: 31 Jul 1910 in St Matthew's, Toxteth,
Liverpool, Lancashire, England
d: 07 Feb 1962 in The Homeopathic Hospital,
Liverpool, Lancashire, England

Ancestry of Ringo Starr's Maternal Grandfather John Gleave

Peter Gleave
b: Warrington, Lancashire, England (Circa 1805)
m: 16 May 1831 in Grappenhall, Cheshire
d: 1877 in Warrington, Lancashire, England

Amelia King
b: 1810 in Manchester, Lancashire, England
d: 1861 in Warrington, Lancashire, England

Thomas Oppenshaw
b: 1791 in Bolton Le Moors, Lancashire, England
m: 02 Aug 1825 in St Nicholas, Liverpool,....
d: Jun 1851 in West Derby, Liverpool,....

Catherine Ann Woods
b: Warrington, Lancashire, England (Circa 1798)

Patrick Conroy
b: Ireland
Occupation: Gardener

Thomas O'Connor
b: Ireland
d: Wherabouts Unknown (Between 1868-90)
Occupation: Stonemason

William Gleave
b: 1835 in Warrington, Lancashire, England
m: 04 Jul 1863 in St Brides, Toxteth, Liverpool, England
d: Jan 1912 in 100 Roselyn Street, Toxteth, Liverpool, England
Occupation: Brick Maker

Mary Oppenshaw
b: 1834 in Norfolk Street, Toxteth, Liverpool, England
d: Sep 1907 in 10 South Street, Toxteth, Liverpool, England

William Conroy
b: Ireland (Circa 1847)
m: 25 Oct 1868 in St Mary's Roman Catholic Church, Edmund Street Liverpool, England
d: 1889 in Byles Street, Toxteth, Liverpool, England
Occupation: Druggist/Engine Driver

Maria Jane O'Connor
b: Dublin, Ireland (Circa 1847)
d: Liverpool, Lancashire, England (after 1911)
Occupation: Charwoman

William Gleave
b: 19 Mar 1867 in Toxteth, Liverpool, England
m: 10 Jun 1889 in St Michael's, Toxteth, Liverpool, England
d: 1934 in Toxteth, Liverpool, England
Occupation: Boiler Maker

Mary Catherine (Kate) Conroy
b: 07 Nov 1869 in Liverpool, England
d: 1916 in Toxteth, Liverpool, England

John Gleave
b: 11 Apr 1891 in 11 Moville Street, Toxteth, Liverpool, Lancashire, England
m: 12 Apr 1914 in St Matthews, Toxteth, Liverpool, England
d: 1936 in Toxteth, Liverpool, Lancashire, England
Occupation: Boiler Maker/Tin Works Labourer

Ancestry of Ringo Starr's Maternal Grandmother Catherine Martha 'Kitty' Johnson

Magnus Johnson
b: Delting, Shetland, Scotland (Circa 1769)
m: 30 Sep 1806 in Delting, Shetland, Scotland
d: 28 May 1856 in Cole Ness, Delting,.....

Ursula Jameson
b: 05 Apr 1788 in Tagon, Delting, Shetland,.....
d: 23 Mar 1876 in Kurkigarth, Olna Firth,.....

Adam Tait
b: Lunnasting, Shetland, Scotland (Circa 1784)
m: 20 Dec 1810 in Nesting, Shetland, Scotland
d: 02 Jan 1855 in Pund, Voe, Olna Firth,.....

Janet Robertson
b: Lunnasting, Shetland, Scotland (Circa 1787)
d: 09 Apr 1862 in Pund, Voe, Olna Firth,.....
Occupation: Wool Carder and Knitter

Peter Johnson
b: 20 May 1824 in South Voxter, Delting, Shetland, Scotland
m: 03 Jan 1850 in Delting, Shetland, Scotland
Occupation: Seaman

Philias "Philly/Philadelphia" Tait
b: 22 Oct 1818 in Lunnasting, Shetland, Scotland
Occupation: Servant in Thomson household (1841)/Worsted Spinner (1851 Census)

James Cunningham
d: County Down, Ireland or Liverpool, Lancashire, England (Before 1881)
Occupation: Gardener

Elizabeth
b: 1818 in County Down, Ireland or Faversham, Kent, England
d: Nov 1911 in 18 Tavistock Street, Toxteth, Liverpool, Lancashire, England

Andrew Johnson
b: 02 Jan 1852 in Delting, Shetland, Scotland
m: 14 Apr 1875 in St Thomas, Toxteth, Liverpool, Lancashire, England
d: Sep 1927 in 18 Tavistock Steet, Toxteth, Liverpool, Lancashire, England
Occupation: Merchant Seaman/Mariner

Mary Elizabeth "Minnie" Cunningham
b: Rostrevor, County Down, Ireland (Circa 1851)

Catherine Martha 'Kitty' Johnson
b: 28 Apr 1891 in 34 Gaskill Street, Toxteth, Liverpool, Lancashire, England
m: 12 Apr 1914 in St Matthews, Toxteth, Liverpool, England
d: 1966 in Toxteth, Liverpool, Lancashire, England

Ancestry of Andrew Johnson

John Johnson
b: Shetland, Scotland (Circa 1740)
Occupation: Fisherman

Catherine Arthurson
b: Shetland, Scotland (Circa 1740)

Thomas Jameson
b: Shetland, Scotland (Circa 1760)
m: 11 Aug 1783 in Delting, Shetland, Scotland
d: before 1841

Margaret Williamson
b: Shetland, Scotland (Circa 1760)
d: after 1841

Jermiah Tait
Occupation: Fisherman

Mary Tulloch

Robert Robertson
Occupation: Fisherman

Martha Thomason

Magnus Johnson
b: Delting, Shetland, Scotland (Circa 1769)
m: 30 Sep 1806 in Delting, Shetland, Scotland
d: 28 May 1856 in Cole Ness, Delting, Shetland, Scotland
Occupation: Farmer

Ursula Jameson
b: 05 Apr 1788 in Tagon, Delting, Shetland, Scotland
d: 23 Mar 1876 in Kurkigarth, Olna Firth, Delting, Shetland, Scotland

Adam Tait
b: Lunnasting, Shetland, Scotland (Circa 1784)
m: 20 Dec 1810 in Nesting, Shetland, Scotland
d: 02 Jan 1855 in Pund, Voe, Olna Firth, Delting, Shetland, Scotland
Occupation: Labourer

Janet Robertson
b: Lunnasting, Shetland, Scotland (Circa 1787)
d: 09 Apr 1862 in Pund, Voe, Olna Firth, Delting, Shetland, Scotland
Occupation: Wool Carder and Knitter

Peter Johnson
b: 20 May 1824 in South Voxter, Delting, Shetland, Scotland
m: 03 Jan 1850 in Delting, Shetland, Scotland
Occupation: Seaman

Philias "Philly/Philadelphia" Tait
b: 22 Oct 1818 in Lunnasting, Shetland, Scotland
Occupation: Servant in Thomson household (1841)/Worsted Spinner (1851 Census)

Andrew Johnson
b: 02 Jan 1852 in Delting, Shetland, Scotland
m: 14 Apr 1875 in St Thomas, Toxteth, Liverpool, Lancashire, England
d: Sep 1927 in 18 Tavistock Steet, Toxteth, Liverpool, Lancashire, England
Occupation: Merchant Seaman/Mariner

[126]

Epilogue

As this examination of the Beatles and their ancestry now draws to a close, what, if any, wider conclusions can be drawn?

Certainly, there are marked similarities in all their trees.

All four Beatles are tied to the land, having farmers in their immediate ancestry, not at all surprising given the relatively recent status of Liverpool as a city. Many of the inhabitants will have been attracted there from the surrounding countryside, a nationwide trend at the same time Liverpool began to transform into an international dock, with industrialisation transforming Britain's essentially rural 18th century society to a patchwork of urbanised towns and cities by the mid-19th

All the Beatles also have ancestors involved in one way on the sea or docks, again hardly surprising given Liverpool's status as a major port city. These include Sail Makers, Boswains, Ship Wrights, Bell Boys, Stewards, Mariners and Sailors.

Lennon and McCartney both have great-grandfathers, William Stanley and James McCartney, who in the same decade, the 1880s, left settled and respectable occupations, Lennon's as a Clerk, McCartney's as a Plumber and Painter, and took to a life on the sea, leaving their wives and children at home alone. Both took this decision relatively late in life, in their late thirties, suggesting this perhaps was the equivalent of a midlife crisis for Liverpool men of the time, who, after years of watching ships leave port from the sidelines, yearned to see some of the world for themselves. Whatever the truth, life on the sea was no easy adventure, it was tough and potentially ruinous to those not raised to it, and tellingly, both men had returned permanently to dry land within a decade of their decision.

All four Beatles share Coopers, Carpenters and Joiners as ancestors, again not surprising in a dock city where such skilled craftsmen were in constant high demand.

Perhaps more surprisingly, three of the four Beatles also have Inn-Keepers and Publicans as ancestors, though only Ringo's within the city of Liverpool, his Scottish 3 x great-grandmother, Marion Foggo, running the *Dumfries and Galloway Inn* there, whereas George had ancestors running taverns in South Wales, and Paul has Victorian Inn-keeping ancestors in England's Midlands.

At least three of the four Beatles, Ringo, George and John, have military ancestors, Ringo and George's grandfathers both serving during the First World War, with George's grandfather sadly making the ultimate sacrifice having fallen in service. John, the committed pacifist, who famously wrote *'I Don't Wanna be a Soldier'*, was the great-great grandson of a career soldier Charles Gildea, who spent the best years of his life under the King's Shilling.

The same three Beatles, Ringo, George and John also share Stonemasons and Builders for ancestors. Ringo and George both have Engine Drivers as ancestors, whereas as Ringo and Paul both share Boiler Makers. Whilst not exclusive to dock cities, both these occupations were certainly important trades there.

All four Beatles have Professional Gardeners as direct ancestors, in John and George's case both employed on the landed estates of British aristocratic families.

All of the above occupations perhaps fall well into the definition of Working Class Artisans, though certainly Ringo's ancestors had achieved some degree of social respectability through the lucrative Stone Mason's trade, describing themselves as 'Gentlemen' in the records and owning their own homes in Toxteth, where his family were long settled.

John Lennon is perhaps notable as the only Beatle with several White-Collar Workers, Clerks, on both sides of his immediate family tree, who would perhaps have considered themselves more aligned to the aspiring 'Middle Classes' rather than the 'Working Classes', and he undoubtedly has some very prosperous ancestry further back in time on his Welsh line.

That said all four Beatles, John included, had ancestors who would have been no strangers to poverty and real hardship, the like of which are largely unknown to us today, and are difficult to fully comprehend. This is evidenced by the fact at least three band members, John, Paul and George, all have direct ancestors who ended their days in the Union Workhouse, the much-feared scourge of the Victorian poor.

Perhaps surprisingly few are any ancestors recorded working as musicians. Though family tales suggest several of the Beatles' ancestors had strong musical inclinations, in most cases this seems not to have risen above hobby. Certainly, Paul McCartney's father, Joe, for a time pushed towards the professional touring in his own jazz band, and John Lennon's father Fred, an occasional crooner on the cruise ships where he worked as a Steward, made a belated attempt at a music career, late in life, on the back of his son's fame, in the 1960s.

Further back than this though, it is only John's maternal ancestors who show any sustained predilection for the creative arts, great-grandfather, William Henry Stanley, recorded working professionally as a Musician at the turn of the 20th century, and his father in turn recorded working as an Actor, though what form or scope that may have taken is for the time being unclear.

Despite this it may nevertheless just be possible, with varying degrees of imagination, to see shades of the future talents of the four Beatles and some indication of the source of those talents reflected in the various occupations followed by their ancestors.

For example, Ringo's ancestors were particularly involved in the trade of Boiler Making, for several generations, the art of beating and shaping metal with hammer, involving strong and capable hands. George's Harrison ancestors on the other hand were master craftsmen, long involved in Carpentry, the art of delicately and lovingly working for hours on end with individual pieces of wood to create something new and special from them. Out of all four band members John's ancestors show a particular predominance for making their living by pen and paper, at least one of his ancestors, the Reverend Richard Farrington, a noted Author and composer of church sermons, perhaps suggestive of his own later skill as both Poet and Wordsmith.

Moving away from occupation and social status, all four Beatles are again further linked together by their shared Irish ancestry. All four have Irish ancestors on both mother and father's side, in total descending together from at least twenty-six separate Irish immigrants to England and Scotland in the 19th century (See 'Addendum a' for a further detailed view).

Irish heritage is the dominant strain in their ancestry for both John and Paul, who have around 50% Irish genes, compared to just a quarter that trace back in England, the land of their birth. George and Ringo are slightly less Irish in their overall ancestry, though both nevertheless still have around a third of their recent family history traceable back there.

Further still their ancestors in Ireland, with the exception of George's Ffrench family in the South of the Isle, and Paul's Danhers from Limerick in the West, come from a relatively small geographic area, concentrated in the East and North East, with John, Paul and Ringo all sharing ancestors hailing, coincidentally, from the same Northern Irish town of Newry, County Down, or its near environs.

Again, given the geography of the isle this may not be totally surprising, with Liverpool just a short hop across the sea from this area, and the port of Newry being particularly well connected to Liverpool for much of its history, through trade links.

As well as their shared Irish and English links, George and Paul both also have Manx ancestry, Paul having as much Manx as English blood in his veins. Similarly, John could claim as much Welsh blood as English, though it is perhaps surprising given the very short distance of Liverpool from Wales, that in this he is unique amongst the Beatles. George and Ringo can both trace back family roots North of the border to Scotland, though surprisingly none of Paul's ancestral lines ultimately wind back there, his current adopted homeland, for which he holds a great and lasting fondness,

Perhaps the primary link though is the city of Liverpool itself. George, Ringo and Paul can trace ancestry there at least back to the early to mid-18th century. John's ancestors were comparative late comers, though his 4 x great-grandparents, Lynch Bridge and Catherine Sanders, were married there as early as 1790, his first Liverpool ancestors to permanently settle did not arrive until the Great Famine of Ireland 1845-9, though few would argue his credentials as a Scouser nonetheless, a favourite son of the city, with an airport named in his honour.

Once in Liverpool they were never too far from each other, the immigrant McCartneys and Lennons both settling initially in the crowded area bordering the city docks, around the Irish enclave of '*Scottie*' Road. Though they arrived at different times, in different circumstance, for at least one point in the 1870s John Lennon's teenage grandfather Jack lived almost opposite to Paul McCartney's grandfather Joe, then a child of five or six. Did they ever meet one another?

In yet another quirk of fate George's ancestors made their home for over half a century on the same street and even occupied the very same house where John Lennon's ancestors had lived and died, in a small otherwise unremarkable corner of Liverpool's Old Swan district. An uncanny coincidence, which could lead one to ponder the wider paths of fate perhaps at work in the world.

In overview, the story of the Beatles ancestry is in many ways the wider story of Liverpool itself, and in retelling it here it has hopefully shone some small light not just on the *'Fab Four'*, but on that special city itself, giving a tiny snapshot to the colour and vibrancy of a place and community which through these four favoured sons shone a light into the world with their music, a light that has scarcely dimmed, and which continues to enrich generation after generation who discover and embrace it.

Ultimately, we have these ancestors who paved the way to thank for that, and the city itself which nurtured and created them, they all played their own part, however small, in the wider Beatles story, and this work has been, as a dedicated fan, my own small act of gratitude for that not inconsiderable legacy.

Richard A Edmunds

January 2018

[129]

Irish Ancestry of the Beatles

Below is a summarised breakdown of the Irish Ancestry of the four Beatles, an area which has been of particular interest to previous researchers:

John Lennon - 9 Irish Immigrants to Britain

- 2 x great-grandmother **Bridget Farley,** born October 1803, at Nobber (An Obair), County Meath, Ireland.

- 2 x great-grandfather **James McConville,** born circa 1810, in County Down, Ireland.

- 2 x great-grandfather **Roger Maguire,** born Dec 1810, in Whitewood, Nobber (An Obair), County Meath, Ireland.

- 2 x great-grandmother **Bridget Torley,** born circa 1811, in County Down, Ireland.

- 2 x great-grandmother **Ann Rogers,** born circa 1820, in County Tyrone, Ireland.

- Great-grandfather **James Lennon,** born circa 1829, in County Down, Ireland.

- Great-grandmother **Jane McConville,** born May 1831, in Newry, County Down, Ireland.

- Great-grandfather **James Maguire,** born May 1840, in Whitewood, Nobber (An Obair), County Meath, Ireland.

- Great-grandmother **Elizabeth Jane Gildea** born 1846, in Drumragh, Omagh, County Tyrone, Ireland.

Paul McCartney - 8 Irish Immigrants to Britain

- 3x great-grandfather **James McCartney,** born circa 1787, in Newry, County, Down, Ireland.

- 3x great-grandmother **Ann Rooney,** born circa 1800, in Ireland.

- 3x great-grandfather **James Hughes,** born circa 1793, in Ireland.

- 3x great-grandmother **Alice McCardell,** born circa 1805, in Ireland.

- 2x great-grandmother **Rosanna Hughes,** born circa 1828, in Ireland.

- Great-grandfather **John Danaher,** born in 1841, in Limerick, County Limerick, Ireland.

- Grandfather **Owen Mohin,** born 19th January 1880, in Tullynamalra, Lough Egish, County Monaghan, Ireland.

Ringo Starr - 5 Irish Immigrants to Britain

- 4 x great-grandfather **Francis Steele,** born circa 1770, in Ireland.

- 2x great-grandfather **Thaddeus John Edward James,** born circa 1833, in Ireland.

- 2 x great-grandfather **William Conroy,** born circa 1847, in Ireland.

- 2x great-grandmother **Maria Jane O'Connor,** born circa 1847, in Dublin, Ireland.

- Great-grandmother **Mary Elizabeth 'Minnie' Cunningham,** born circa 1851, in Rostrevor, County Down, Ireland.

George Harrison - 4 Irish Immigrants to Britain

- 4x great-grandfather **Andrew Thomson,** born circa 1761, in Ireland.

- 3 x great-grandfather **John Duff,** born circa 1799, in Ireland.

- 3 x great-grandmother **Jane Anderson,** born circa 1806, in Ireland.

- Grandfather **John Ffrench,** born 31st March 1870, in Ferns, County Wexford, Ireland.

John Lennon's Royal Ancestry

[**Foreword**: I decided to reproduce detail of John Lennon's possible connection with the Royal Families of Wales here in the addendum rather than the main body of the work, principally because I have doubts as to the accuracy of the claim. Though I am satisfied, from my own research, that John Lennon was the 9-x great-grandson of William Owen of Cefnysgwyd, Llechylched, Anglesey, a Welsh land owner who lived in the early 17th century, William's own descent back to the Welsh princes of Medieval and Norman Wales, detailed below, I have not personally researched in the original sources, and this account is primarily based on previous printed accounts of his genealogy given in J.E. Griffith's 1914 work *'Pedigree of Anglesey and Caernarvonshire Families p.321/2',* *' Miscellania Genealogica et Heraldica'* published in 1892, and the online resource *'Welsh Medieval Database Primarily of Nobility and Gentry'.* I make no statement to the absolute truth of the claim below and leave it to the reader and future researchers to judge the veracity, or otherwise, of the details set out below.]

John Lennon's 6 x great-grandfather, the Reverend Richard Farringdon, was the son of Robert Farringdon, a Vintner of Bridge Street, Chester, born and baptised in March 1702. His wife Elizabeth Jones, born in Anglesey, Wales, is recorded as the heiress of her grandfather William Owen, born circa 1605, when she sold her remaining rights over his estate in 1702.

Several genealogies claim William Owen was the grandson of Owain ap Huw (1518-1613), who twice served as High Sheriff of Anglesey during the reign of Queen Elizabeth I. His wife Elsbeth Gruffyd, was the daughter of his maternal uncle Elise ap Morus (1493-1571), the Deputy High Sheriff of Merioneth and Catrine Stanley, daughter of Piers Stanley of Ewloe, Flintshire, High Sheriff of Merioneth, a great-grandson of Sir William Stanley of Hooton, Cheshire. Owain ap Huw also descended from this 14th century English Knight through his father's line, detailed below, so if this information is correct it would make John Lennon twice descended from the aristocratic Stanley family of Northern England.

As first cousins, both Owain ap Huw and wife Elsbeth Gruffyd, claim descent through their respective parents, to Tudur ap Gruffudd "aka *Fychan*", Lord of Gwyddelwern, brother of Owain Glyndwr, the Welsh rebel leader crowned Prince of Wales in the opening decades of the 15th century. Tudur was killed at the Battle of Pwll Melyn on 5th May 1405, aged forty-two, fighting in Owain's uprising against King Henry IV and English rule in Wales. His resemblance to his brother was so great initially the English believed they had slain Owain himself, and his head was decapitated and publicly displayed. If this genealogy is correct Tudur would be John Lennon's 17 x great-grandfather.

Owain and Tudur based their claim to rule an independent Wales, both on their descent from the royal house of the Princes of Powys, through their father Gruffudd Fychan II, Lord of Glyndyfrdwy and Cynllaith, ninth in decent from Bleddyn ap Cynfyn, King of Gwynedd & Powyss 1063–1075, and the royal house of Deheubarth through their mother, Elen ferch Tomas ap Llywelyn, ninth in descent from Rhys ap Tewdwr, King of Deheubarth 1078–1093, ancestor of the later 16th century Royal House of Tudor of England and Wales.

Even without this link to the Tudors, John Lennon's ancestry can still be traced back through the same posited ancestor, 11 x great-grandfather, Owain ap Hugh, to the Royal Houses of both England and Scotland.

Through the male line, Owain also descends from Llywelyn the Great, perhaps the most famous of all the Welsh Kings. If correct he would be John Lennon's 25 x great-grandfather. Llywelyn's wife was a daughter of King John of England, and through this link Lennon's probable ancestry traces back a further four generations to William the Conqueror and King Malcolm III of Scotland, of Shakespearean *Macbeth* fame, both of whom would be great-grandfathers, thirty generations removed.

Through William the Conqueror's ancestry John can be traced even further back to the 9th century Vikings of Scandinavia who founded the colony of Normandy in France, and through Malcolm's wife, Queen Margaret of Scotland, to the earliest, Anglo-Saxon, rulers of England. In Margaret, Lennon also has a canonised saint in his tree. A granddaughter of King Edmund Ironside of England, she was awarded this honour two centuries after her death, by Pope Innocent IV, in recognition of her *'Personal holiness, fidelity to the Church, work for religious reform, and charity'*. Through her Lennon would be a 37 x great-grandson of King Alfred the Great of England, and thirty nine generations removed from Egbert of Wessex, most often thought of as the first true King of England.

13th century depiction of England's first King Egbert of Wessex

John Winston Ono Lennon (1940-1980)

|

Julia Stanley (1914-1958)

|

Annie Jane Millward (1873-1941)

|

Mary Elizabeth Morris (1851-1932)

|

William Morris (1825-1879)

|

Elizabeth Bridge (1795-1854)

|

Lynch Bridge (1765-1847)

|

Mary Farrington (c.1733-1808)

|

Rev. Richard Farrington (1702-1772)

|

Elizabeth Jones (c.1675)

|

Catrin Owen (c.1640)

|

William Owen (c.1605)

|

Richard Owen (c.1570)

|

Owain *ap* Huw (c.1518-1613) *(see fig.1a & b)* **+ Elsbeth Gruffyd (c.1530)** *(see fig.2)*

[134]

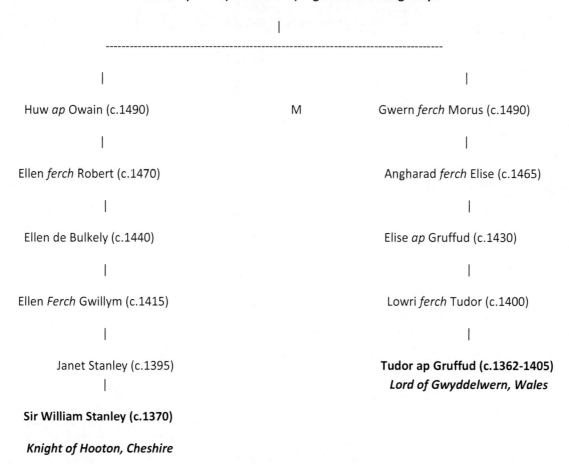

Owain *ap* Huw (c.1518-1613) High Sheriff of Anglesey

Huw *ap* Owain (c.1490) M Gwern *ferch* Morus (c.1490)

Ellen *ferch* Robert (c.1470) Angharad *ferch* Elise (c.1465)

Ellen de Bulkely (c.1440) Elise *ap* Gruffud (c.1430)

Ellen *Ferch* Gwillym (c.1415) Lowri *ferch* Tudor (c.1400)

Janet Stanley (c.1395) **Tudor ap Gruffud (c.1362-1405)**
  Lord of Gwyddelwern, Wales

Sir William Stanley (c.1370)

Knight of Hooton, Cheshire

(fig. 2)

Elsbeth Gruffyd (c.1530) wife of Owain *ap* Hugh

|

| |

Elise *ap* Morus (c.1493-1571)   M.   Catrine Stanley (c.1495)

| |

Angharad *ferch* Elise (c.1465)   Piers Stanley III (c.1460)

| |

Elise *ap* Gruffud (c.1430)   Piers Stanley II (c.1430)

| |

Lowri *ferch* Tudor (c.1400)   Piers Stanley I (c.1400)

| |

Tudor *ap* Gruffud (c.1362-1405)   **Sir William Stanley (c.1370)**

Lord of Gwyddelwern, Wales   *Knight of Hooton, Cheshire*

(fig, 1b)

Owain *ap* Huw (c.1518-1613), *High Sheriff of Anglesey*

|

Huw *ap* Owain (c.1490)

|

Owain *ap* Meuraig (c.1465)

|

Meuraig *ap* Llywelyn (c.1440)

|

Llywelyn *ap* Hwlcyn (c.1420)

|

Hwlcyn *ap* Hywel (c.1400)

|

Angharad *ferch* Hywel (c.1375)

|

Margred *ferch* Gruffudd *"Gôch"* (c.1350)

|

Efa *ferch* Ieuan (c.1325)

|

Gwenllian *ferch* Gronwy "*Llwyd*" (c.1300)

|

Lleucu *ferch* Madog (c.1275)

|

Madog *ab* Elise, *Lord of Llangar* (c.1255)

|

Annes *ferch* Dafydd (c.1235)

[137]

|

Dafydd *ap* Llywelyn *"Mawr", Prince of Wales* (c.1215-1246)

|

Llywelyn the Great (1173-1240)   M.   **Joan of England (1191-1237)** *(see fig 3)*

Prince of Aberffraw, Lord of Snowdon   *Princess of Wales, Lady of Snowdon*

(fig.3)

Joan of England (1191-1237)

|

King John of England (1166-1216)

|

King Henry II of England (1133-1189)

|

Queen Matilda of England (1102-1167)

|

King Henry I of England (c.1068-1135)   M.   Matilda of Scotland (c1080-1118)

| |

King William I *'The Conqueror'* (c.1028-1087)   **King Malcolm III of Scotland (1031-1093)**

M.

Margaret of Scotland (c. 1045 – 1093) *(see fig. 4)*

(fig. 4)

St Margaret of Scotland (c. 1045 – 1093)

|

Edward the Exile (1016 – 1057)

|

Edmund *'Ironside'*, King of England (c.988-1016)

|

Ethelred *'the Unready'*, King of England (c.968-1016)

|

Edgar *'the Peaceful'*, King of England (943-975)

|

Edmund I, King of England (939-946)

|

Edward *'the Elder'*, King of England (899-924)

|

Alfred the Great, King of England (849-899)

|

Aethulwulf of Wessex, King of England (c.800-858)

|

Egbert of Wessex, 1st King of England (c.770-839)

Owain *ap* Meuraig and his wife, Elin *ferch* Robert, circa 1490, depicted on the stained-glass windows of St Cadwaladr Church, Llangadwaladr, Anglesey, Wales. Owain fought at the Battle of Bosworth Field in 1485, to install his Welsh kinsman, Henry Tudor, as King of England. According to the above genealogy he and Elin would be 13 x great-grandparents to John Lennon.

[140]

Maggie May: The Story of a Liverpool Classic

Oh, dirty Maggie May they have taken her away
And she'll never walk down Lime Street any more
Oh the judge he guilty found her
For robbing a homeward bounder
That dirty no good robbin' Maggie May
To the port of Liverpool
There she turned me tool,
Two pounds ten a week, that was my pay

One of the more idiosyncratic entries in the Beatles oeuvre, appearing on their last album *Let it Be*, *Maggie May* was recorded as a 38-second ad-lib between takes of *Two of Us*. It was in keeping with the theme of nostalgia and lasting friendship contained in the latter song, having been performed by John Lennon and his school Skiffle group the *Quarrymen* on 6th July 1957, at St Peter's Church Fete, in Walton, the fateful day he first met the fifteen-year-old Paul McCartney *(pictured above)*.

A traditional Liverpool folk song, sometimes referred to as a second anthem of the city, it relates the tale of a notorious street walker, Maggie May, who supplemented her nefarious income by robbing her clients, resulting in her conviction and transportation to a British penal colony, in some versions Van Diemen's Land, modern day Tasmania, in others the colony at Botany Bay, modern Sydney.

[141]

It has been claimed the song is based on a true story and that its original composition occurred during the era of Australian transportation (*1788-1868*). As evidence of this Stan Hugill (*1906-1992*) the most notable 20th century historian of sea shanties, referenced an early version, clearly a fore runner of the same song, entitled *Nelly Ray* which appeared in print in a 1930 London nautical publication *Blue Peter*.

Nelly Ray. (Song.)

I was paid off at the home,
From a voyage to Sierra Leone;
Three pounds monthly, was my pay.
When I drew the cash I grinned,
But I very soon got skinned
By a lass who lived in Peter Street, called Ray.

I shall ne'er forget the day
When I met Nellie Ray.
'Twas at the corner of the Canning Place;
With a mighty crin-o-line
Like a frigate of the line,
As if I were a slaver she gave chase.

Saying, *'What cheer ! homeward bounder,*
Just you come along with me';
So in Peter Street we had some gin and tea;
It was morn when I awoke
Then I found that I was broke
For sweet Nellie had skedaddled with my money.

To the magistrate I went,
Where I stated my lament :
They soon had poor Nelly in the Dock.
And the Judge he guilty found her,
For she'd robbed a homeward bounder,
And he sent her to Van Dieman's far away.

Oh! my charming Nellie Ray,
They have taken you away,
You have gone to Van Diemen's cruel shore;
For you've skinned so many tailors,
And you've robbed so many sailors,
That we'll look for you in Peter Street no more.

It appears at the very end of an article which reproduced the journal of Charles Picknell (*1810-1886*) a mariner of Hastings, Sussex, who served in the Royal Navy from 1825-1851, and afterwards until his death, held the post of Pier Warden at Hastings. The journal recalled a voyage he made to Australia in summer 1830 as a junior crew member of the *Kains* convict ship.

The *Kains* carried 120 convicted felons, all female, and two thirds aged between fourteen and thirty. The ships medic, Doctor Clarke, described the women of the *Kains* in his journal   -

The general character and conduct of the prisoners were such as might be expected from the lowest class of society - from persons whom all the wise and salutary laws of England had failed to reclaim, most immoral and abandoned, if there ever was a Hell afloat it must have been in the shape of a female convict ship, quarrelling, fighting, thieving, destroying in private each other's property for a mean spirit of devilishness - conversation with each other most abandoned without feeling or shame. As regarded the personal cleanliness of the prisoners that in some measure depended on their natural disposition, education and attitude, some of them by nature and habit were cleanly while others were filthy to the 90th degree.

Picknell's own journal concentrates on the twenty-six-man crew of which he was a member, most of whom spent a large part of the journey drunk and singing *'saucy songs'* below decks. Though *Nelly Ray* is presented as an example of one such song, it is unclear whether it was an example cited by Picknell himself in the original journal or added later due to its relevance to the subject matter, female transportation. It appears at the very end of the journal after a few additional notes on the journal by Picknell and after a list of provisions held on the *Kains*. The original journal itself apparently no longer survives to indicate one way or the other.

If the song was related by Picknell, it is extremely doubtful it was heard on the original 1830 voyage. Chief among the objections to this dating is the fact it makes reference to the unlucky sailor being *'paid off at the home'*. This must surely refer to the Liverpool Sailors' Home, in Canning Place, also referenced in the song, an institute which first opened its doors a full two decades later in 1850.

The language used in this version also raises several alarm bells. The word *'Skedaddled'* did not enter the general lexicon until the early 1860s, when it was coined by the Union side in the American Civil War. A search into the *British Newspaper Archive 1710-1953* confirms it was unknown in the British Isles before this date, first appearing in print an Irish Newspaper in May 1862, in the context of American civil war forces. A craze for its usage then occurred with it over a thousand appearances in various different British newspapers in the remaining months of that year alone, with it explicitly stated to be a new word of American origin.

The term *'Homeward bounder'*, which appears in Picknell's version, and with such regularity in all known versions of the song that it was surely present from inception, similarly does not appear anywhere in print, newspaper or book, until 1835, a full five years after the *Kains* voyage, and, remained exceedingly rare until popularised in the 1850s *(as the instances of its usage in British Newspapers 1710-1900, below, show)*. It then fell out of favour as an archaic term, until a brief resurgence of popularity in the 1890s.

1830s = 6	**1860s** = 44	**1890s** = 52
1840s = 10	**1870s** = 40	
1850s = 302	**1880s** = 19	

The verses *'With a mighty crin-o-line, Like a frigate of the line'* similarly points to a later date as Crinoline petticoats did not become generally available or popular until the 1840s, and furthermore, frigate warships rigged with so-called *crinoline frames*, nets to deter torpedo fire, were unknown until 1877.

A search of Liverpool newspapers for the term *'frigate of the line'* or *'frigate on the line'* in the 19th century shows it is also entirely absent in the 1830s. It then gradually creeps into use, appearing twice in the 1840s, six times in the 1850s, eight times in the 1860s, once in the 1870s and then disappearing entirely for the remainder of the decade. Though hardly scientific, this nevertheless suggests it was terminology more common in the 1850s-60s, and rarely used before or after.

[143]

H.M.S Hotspur rigged with a *'crinoline frame'* torpedo net, circa 1879.

The metaphor of *Nelly Ray* as a British war frigate is extended further with the line *'As if I were a slaver she gave chase'*. This also seems an ill fit with the proposed 1830 dating, as the general blockade of the African slave trade commenced with the 1842 Webster–Ashburton Treaty, an agreement between the British and U.S government to work together on the abolition of the slave trade. (*Britain was later granted full authority to intercept American slave ships in 1861, by the Lincoln administration, and the Royal Navy squadron remained busy in this endeavour until 1870.*)

Though these factors do not rule out Charles Picknell noting the song in his journal, it does indicate that if so, it was an addition made later in his life, after 1877 at the earliest. Further support for this theory is the rate of sailor's pay, cited in the song as *'three pounds monthly'*. This British Newspaper Archive indicates this was typical sailors pay in the decade 1880-1890. For example, an article in the March 1884 *London Standard* records that for *'three pounds a month sailors have the chance of procuring employment off any shore'*. A later article entitled *Our Sailors* printed in the *Liverpool Mercury* of 3rd February 1890 relates *'These sailors had shipped in the "Thorn" for a voyage to Australia and back, and they were to get three pounds a month, with, of course, their board and lodging.'*

So, if *Maggie May* was not a genuine product of the transportation era, just what are the songs true origins?

That both the form and content of the song show obvious similarities to the American Minstrel standard *Darling Nelly Gray* has long been recognised and acknowledged, and the fact that the earliest known version reproduced in the *Blue Peter* is sung in honour of a *Charming Nelly Ray* would seem to indicate it has its origin as a bawdy comic parody of the former.

One of the earliest recorded discussions as to the origins of *Maggie May* appears in the 1955 edition of *Sea Breezes: The Magazine of Ships and the Sea* (published in Old Hall Street, Liverpool). There an ex sailor, who began his sea career in 1913 working as an engineer on the *'Ella Sayer'* of Newcastle, recalled hearing *Maggie May* sung by his stoke hold crew while perched on planks painting down the engine, describing them as *'good firemen, good beer drinkers, and good singers!'*. Another former seaman questioned the identity of the songs protagonist as he recalled a version of what was clearly in every other respect the same song, sung five years earlier, in the winter of 1908 by one of his shipmates on the barque *Pharos*, bound for Australia, but in this version, as in Picknell's, the song instead referred to a *Charming Nelly Ray*.

[144]

Darling Nelly Gray certainly shows many similarities to *Charming Nelly Ray/Maggie May* not just in melody, form and content but also in its related themes of enforced bondage and geographic separation. Composed by Benjamin Russel Hanby *(1833-1866)*, an American educationalist and pastor, in the year 1856, it is a moving and mournful lament of a Kentucky slave, parted from his beloved, when she is sold south to the harsh Georgian cotton fields. It recounts their pain at separation and their eventual post-death reunion in the afterlife:

Darling Nelly Gray (Benjamin Hanby)

There's a low, green valley, on the old Kentucky shore.
Where I've whiled many happy hours away,
A-sitting and a-singing by the little cottage door,
Where lived my darling Nelly Gray.

(Chorus)
Oh! my poor Nelly Gray, they have taken you away,
And I'll never see my darling anymore;
I'm sitting by the river and I'm weeping all the day.
For you've gone from the old Kentucky shore.

When the moon had climbed the mountain and the stars were shining too.
Then I'd take my darling Nelly Gray,
And we'd float down the river in my little red canoe,
While my banjo sweetly I would play.

One night I went to see her, but *"She's gone!"* the neighbours say.
The white man bound her with his chain;
They have taken her to Georgia for to wear her life away,
As she toils in the cotton and the cane.

My canoe is under water, and my banjo is unstrung;
I'm tired of living anymore;
My eyes shall look downward, and my song shall be unsung
While I stay on the old Kentucky shore.

My eyes are getting blinded, and I cannot see my way.
Hark! there's somebody knocking at the door.
Oh! I hear the angels calling, and I see my Nelly Gray.
Farewell to the old Kentucky shore.

(Chorus)
Oh, my darling Nelly Gray, up in heaven there they say,
That they'll never take you from me anymore.
I'm a-coming-coming-coming, as the angels clear the way,
Farewell to the old Kentucky shore!

The song was universally popular from inception. It was bought to England by *Christy's Minstrels* in 1859 where newspapers first note it as *Nelly Gray* a *'beautiful little song'* in December of that year. The *Liverpool Daily Post* of 31st January 1860 makes note of its debut performance in their city by the same American Minstrel troupe, *"We must specially notice the exquisitely charming song of "Nelly Gray" beautiful, from its very simplicity, given with remarkable expression of feeling".*

It remained popular for decades afterwards, and by 1884 there are reports it was on occasion being popularly sung alternatively both as *My Charming Nellie Gray* and *Charming Nelly Ray:*

Some capital times were rendered upon handbells. The brothers *'Charming Nelly Gray'* and *'The Chimes'* receiving rounds of applause – *South London Press 10th May 1884*

"*My Charming Nellie Gray, They have taken you away, - And I'll never see my darling any more"* Was heard on every side. and voiced by all sorts – *Lloyd's Weekly Newspaper, 29th March 1896*

'*Charming Nelly Ray'* and various other charmers were duly the sound of the choruses reverberating the distant hills of Kent. – *Maidstone Journal and Kentish Advertiser, 11th August 1898*

If Charles Picknell's journal is taken at face value as entirely his own work, (it of course remains possible the song was added after his death by whoever inherited the diary) then it at least proves that an alternate version of *Darling Nelly Gray* sung as *Charming Nelly Ray* did exist by the time of his death in 1886, and that by extension, both versions, the haunting original and the comic parody, co-existed at that time, perhaps accounting for this late confusion in newspapers.

The first specific reference to a song named *Charming Nelly Ray* in performance can, however, be dated back to more than a quarter of a century before both these reports, to October 1870, when it formed part of the repertoire of Mr. Edgar Wilding, '*a brisk and agreeable comic vocalist'.*

Wilding, a linen weaver's son, was baptised as Andrew Edgar Wilding in Ashford, Kent, in August 1840. Married at nineteen, he lived with his wife and children in Marylebone, London, and was employed all his working life, like John Lennon's great-grandfather, as a solicitor's clerk.

He began his parallel career as a comic in 1864, styling himself as *The Postman,* appearing on stage in Theatres and Music Halls whilst dressed in a postman's uniform and singing of the people for whom he professed to have letters. This humorous skit remained popular throughout his stage life, (he was still performing it at the termination of his career eight years later in 1872), though he regularly added other popular comedy songs of the day to his repertoire, including *The Mousetrap Man* (1866) *The Irrepressible Donkey* (1868) *Happy Costermonger Bill* (1872) *The Sandstone Girl* (1872) and *Carroty Hair* (1872).

Other contemporary newspaper reports describe him variously as '*A very original and smart comic singer'* '*A funny little man, ludicrous and extremely eccentric', 'An eccentric comic singer of the old school'* and '*A laughably grotesque comic vocalist'.*

Further insight into Wilding's career and personal circumstances appears in the following newspaper report in November 1876:

Wilding/Wilding/Hardy **- Edgar Wilding, a music-hall singer, petitioned for divorce by reason of his wife's adultery with the co-respondent. The marriage took place on November 14th 1859 at All Souls Church, both them that time being under age. She had a little money of her own, and they lived at different places in London, the petitioner being engaged as a clerk to a solicitor. About three years after the marriage he had reason to complain of his wife's mis-conduct, she having given way to intemperate habits in consequence of which he was compelled to separate from her, he undertaking to take care of the children of the marriage, and to allow the respondent keeping each week. At that time, he was engaged as a comic vocalist at provincial music-halls. Subsequently he obtained engagements at some of the London music-halls, which he was compelled to relinquish in consequence of the disturbance which his wife caused at these places. Upon his discovering that she was living with the co-respondent in Crown Street, Soho, he instituted the present suit. Evidence having been given in support of the case Sir James granted a decree nisi and allowed the petitioner to have the custody of the children.**

The divorce papers show the couple had six children together 1860-66, but the marriage broke down *'some time before the year of 1870',* Wilding accusing his wife of living as a *'common prostitute'* and committing adultery with diverse persons unknown to him during this time, and contracting Venereal Disease for which she was treated in the St Pancras Workhouse from September-November 1869.

It was to this backdrop of marital turmoil, that *Charming Nelly Ray* first appears as part of his stage act, as one of four *'brisk and agreeable new comic songs'* debuted in front of a packed audience at The Eastern Music Hall, Limehouse in the week of 9-16th October 1870, (the others being *Selling Laces, Dissolving Views,* and *Wasn't it a funny thing).* At least two of these last three do not appear elsewhere, so may have been his own original compositions, and they evidently proved popular as six weeks later *The Era* newspaper of 27th November 1870 reports that *'Mr. Edgar Wilding, sings some of the best comic songs ever written, in a spirited style, and gratified the people with his songs of "Nellie Ray," "Wasn't that a funny thing for her to say to me," and "Dissolving Views'.*

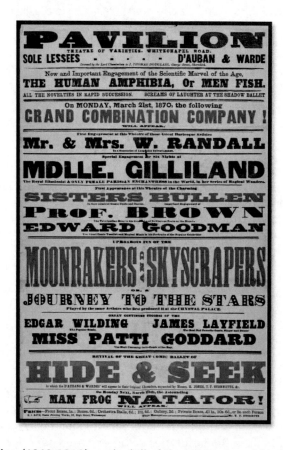

Andrew Edgar Wilding (1840-1910) on the bill of the Whitechapel Pavilion, 21st March 1870.

.

Whether *Nelly Ray* was also of his original composition is open to question. It would seem most likely it was the following song, which later appears in at least two printed broadsheet versions, author unnamed, one that notes that it had been *'sung with success'* by Tom Bournley, a rival comic and song writer who performed in London and various other cities from 1865-1880, and the other that it was sung with *'immense success'* by another London comic, Gus Westbrook, whose stage career similarly overlapped with Wilding's, lasting from 1868-1881:

[147]

NELLY RAY.

I love a little country queen, a village beauty rare,
With rosy cheeks, white pearly teeth and lovely nut-brown air
Her waist is so slender, and her feet they are so small,
Of all the girls I ever loved, my Nelly beats them all.

(chorus) *Nelly Ray, Nelly Ray, charming little Nell,*
Nelly Ray like birds in May, singing all the day,
Nelly Ray, Nelly Ray, pretty little girl;
I never had a sweetheart like my little Nelly Ray.

Her father is a farmer in a village down in Kent,
And being on my holidays, to spend them there I went,
One day while strolling out, up to the farm house I did roam
And there I first saw Nelly, as she drove the cattle home.

I took my Nelly for a walk among the bright green grass,
And words of love I whisper'd then to this sweet country lass;
I sat her down upon a bank, and then sat by her side,
And while my arm was round her waist, she pledged to be my bride.

And now I've named the wedding day and happy we shall be,
No thought of jealousy will cross the mind of her or me;
But in our little- farmhouse we'll be happy night and day.
Our lives will pass like sunshine, for I've got the brightest ray.

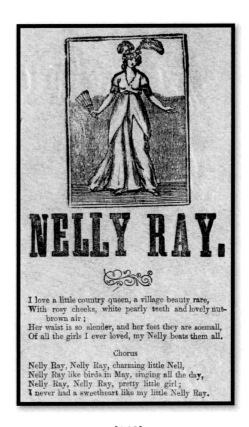

As only Wilding is associated with a song by this same name in contemporary newspaper reports, it's possible he was the original composer, and it was latter covered by his contemporaries Westbrook and Bournley, especially when its content is considered, a love ode to the daughter of a Kent farmer, Wilding of course a Kent lad by birth, spending his formative years there.

However, a year earlier, in November 1869, whilst his wife was confined with her malady to the St Pancras workhouse infirmary, he performed in the north of England, at Durham. His set then included a song entitled *The Returned Convict*. As it *'nearly bought the house down with laughter'* it must have been comic in nature and appears to be his own peculiar rendering of a sombre transportation ballad by the same name, set in Botany Bay, widely popular earlier in the decade from 1859-1865, which begins with the refrain *'Oh well can I remember'*, a stylistic devise which also later appears in *Nelly Ray/Maggie May*.

As Wilding evidently enjoyed some success with this, it just might have provided the impetus to follow up with a reworking of the similarly popular contemporary ballad *Darling Nelly Gray*, in much the same vein, transforming it from a haunting ballad of separated lovers, into a darkly comic tale of transportation, and a prostitute getting her *'just deserts'*, his recent experiences with his errant wife doubtless preying heavy on his mind. If so, it may be his use of *Charming Nelly Ray* as the protagonist was also a deliberate, and not so subtle, dig at his stage rivals Tom Bournley and Gus Westbrook, then enjoying success on the Music Hall scene, perhaps, with the above quoted comic ballad, containing the similar refrain *'Nelly Ray, charming little Nell'*?

A composition date of 1870 for the *Darling Nelly Gray* parody, in any case fits better than an 1830 dating, as it is perhaps the only time the phrases *'Skedaddled' 'Homeward Bounder'* and *'Frigate of the Line'* were all in popular common parlance, and it is also during the era the British Navy were still heavily involved in tracking slavers on the African coast.

During his tour of the north he is specifically credited with tailoring the content of his songs to suite local audiences. The scene of his *Nelly Ray's* debut, The Eastern Music Hall and Hotel, Limehouse, had been built a decade earlier by Charles Dunk, and according to one source *"the building quickly became a haunt for local sailors weaving in and out of the docks"*.

The Eastern Hotel and Music Hall, Limehouse, pictured in the 1890s.

[149]

Providing cheap drink, lodging and entertainment for its transient dockside community, the general character of the venue is apparent from a case heard at the Old Bailey ten months earlier, on 13th December 1869, when Neils Olsen and Thore Neilson , describing themselves through an interpreter as the Master and Mate of the ship *Expedite,* lying in the river, off Limehouse, charged nineteen year old Elizabeth Green, with having violently struck both of them in the bar of *The Eastern Music Hall* stealing from them a watch, chain and locket, which she passed to an accomplice, twenty three year old Henry Newland, and which were later recovered by the police from a dockside pawn shop.

The entire area of the East India Docks was positively awash with sailors, both native and foreign, and was notorious for its opium dens and high level of poverty and vice, another contemporary source complaining that the seamen attracted prostitutes to the area *'like flies to a honey-pot'.*

Five years earlier, in 1865, *An Essay on the Present State of the British Mercantile Marine* bewails the fate of *'homeward bounders'* plied with drink and led astray by *'harpies'* in dock communities, their monthly pay stolen and their clothing disappeared to the pawn shops, all themes that ring with familiarity when considering *Charming Nelly Ray* and its later derivative *Maggie May:*

This being the present state of things, seamen become the easy prey of the *"landsharks"* who surround the " *homeward-bounder* " in every nameable disguise [including] grog shop keepers who under the guise of boarding houses for seaman, lure them into dens of intoxication, profligacy and vice, and first drowning their reason by stupefying drinks, then inflame their passions by every excitement they can place in their way, at length they drain them of every penny of their hard earned gains, and turn them adrift, bodies poisoned, minds disordered by scenes of vice, in which they mingled, (perhaps for the first time), clothing gone, being pledged at the sign of the *'Three Bells'* or at the *'bar'* for drink, leaving them without food, raiment or home, or else they are hurried on board of some ship that may be in want of hands. The month's advance note goes to clear off the old score, it is absorbed by the harpy whose victim he is, not to pay for the sailor's comfortable subsistence, but *'run up'* against him for rum or other viscous indulgences, ruinous to the body and every noble and manly sentiment"

Whether Edgar Wilding's 1870 comic music hall song *Charming Nelly Ray* is the same sweet ode to a Kent farmer's daughter as popularised by his rivals, or the bawdy ode to a transported prostitute by the same name, which later reportedly appears at the conclusion of Charles Picknell's journal, remains an open question, though the latter would certainly match the *'grotesque comic style'* attributed to Wilding by reviewers. If so, the references to crinolines, and their implied similarity to torpedo nets, and the stated rate of the sailor's monthly pay appearing in Picknell's version, may have been later additions and alterations to the song tacked on by sailors in the late 1870s and early 1880s. As pier warden at Hastings, Charles Picknell would have had ample opportunity to hear songs from passing sailors throughout the latter part of his life, and was more likely to have heard it filtered through this source, rather than direct from the London Music Halls.

As Wilding's version of the song was first performed in the capital at Limehouse, not far from Canning Town, for an audience of sailors, *'harpies'* and the surrounding London dockside community, then the references to the Liverpool locations Lime Street and Canning Place, appearing in most versions of the song, may also be later alterations. This cannot be said with certainty though, as in the course of his eight years on the stage, Wilding toured several major cities in England and Scotland, and he had performed at least once in Liverpool, for a week-long engagement in January 1867 at *The Theatre Royal* in Williamson Square. He must then have had a degree of familiarity with the city by the time *Charming Nelly Ray* appeared in his set, and pertinently Williamson Square is directly opposite Peter Street, referenced as the location of Nelly Ray's digs, in the earliest known versions of the song. It is probably also worth noting that at least one other song in Wilding's known repertoire *The Sandstone Girl* was a tongue in cheek romantic ode to a Liverpool girl.

Charming Nelly Ray is only reported to have been performed sporadically on the Music Hall stage after Wilding's own premature retirement, but there is a newspaper report of a Mr T. B. Browning of *The Marionettes* performing *Nelly Ray* a comic song at Ballarat, Victoria, Australia in February 1879, though this more likely refers to the same ode to a Kent farmer's daughter popularised by Wilding's rivals Bournley and Westbrook.

What does seem certain though is a parody version of *Darling Nelly Gray* called *Charming Nelly Ray* existed by the 1890s,and was being sung by sailors in the opening decade of the 20th century. In all likelihood, it had reached audiences the other side of the globe by this point too, where it's transportation theme would have held particular interest, its probable transmission route, the same sailors who comprised both its subject matter and perhaps too, if Wilding was the author, its premier audience. Equally possible, Wilding's bawdy maritime audiences themselves created the parody in the 1870s, from an amalgamation of the popular minstrel ballad *Darling Nelly Gray* and his song *Charming Nelly Ray*. The exact truth, for the time being, remains unclear.

Whoever was the creator, it was not the only parody of *Nelly Gray* then in existence. That songs popularity was so widespread it positively lent itself to the form, with at least two other examples existent in the surviving broadsheets, like *Nelly Ray* both rather dark tales in their subject matter, one revolving around spousal abuse and the other bastardy:

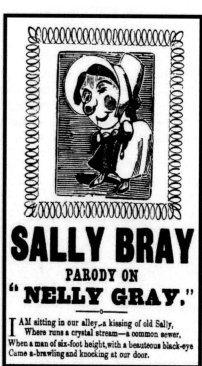

But how then did the comic parody by the name of *Nelly Ray* subsequently morph into *Maggie May*, in some sailor's versions by 1913 at least, and in all latter versions?

Again, the popularity of the *Christy Minstrels* in England, particularly in Liverpool, might account for this. The 19th May 1869 edition of the *Liverpool Mercury* records a further performance in the city by the same troupe which included a rendition of a song *Little Maggie May* which had been '*exquisitely harmonised by Mr. C Blamphin.*

Charles Blamphin (*1830-1895*) a British composer and harpist, originally composed this song in 1864 with the New York born proprietor of his particular band of Christy Minstrels, George Washington '*Pony*' Moore (*1820-1909*). Though Moore is also often referred to as a writer of comic songs and parodies, this particular ditty was very much a sweet saccharine ballad:

LITTLE MAGGIE MAY.
(G.W. Moore and Charles Blamphin 1864)

**The Spring had come, the flowers in bloom, the birds sung out their lay.
Down by a Little running brook I first saw Maggie May.
She had a roguish Jet-black eye, was singing all the day;
And how I loved her, none can tell-my little Maggie May!**

(Chorus)
*My little witching Maggie, Maggie singing all the day;
Oh! how I love her, none can tell, my little Maggie May!*

**Though years rolled on, yet still I loved with heart so light and gay,
And never will this heart deceive my own dear Maggie May.
When others thought that life was gone, and death would take away,
Still by my side did linger one, and that was Maggie May. - Chorus.**

**May Heaven protect me for her sake; I pray, both night and day,
That I, ere long, may call her mine, my own dear Maggie May.
For she is all the world to me, although I'm far away,
I oft times think of the running brook and my little Maggie May. - Chorus.**

As with its earlier contemporary, *Darling Nelly Gray*, *Little Maggie May* is a tale of separated lovers and was equally well received and popular from first debut, even finding itself the subject of a legal dispute in summer 1870 by the composer of *The Sweet Wild Rose* who claimed the theme of the first eight bars were plagiarised.

Legal tussles aside, the following report from April 1887 shows the lasting popularity of *Little Maggie May,* and the importance Moore himself placed on it in building the reputation of his own band of minstrels:

The ceremony took place at the afternoon performance; the gift being acknowledged by Mr. Moore in a few earnest words of thanks to those who had laboured so loyally with him. In addressing the audience, he reminded them that many of the songs in the first part were old ones, which had helped to make the reputation of his troupe, one in particular, entitled "*Maggie May,*" having been written and composed by him more than twenty-five years ago, before he came to London.

Darling Nelly Gray and *Little Maggie May* existed side by side as popular standards of the minstrel repertoire for up to half a century after their first composition. Newspaper evidence show both in contemporary performance as late as 1906, though by then the minstrel craze, and the golden age of the Music Hall in general, had begun to wane.

Though Moore and Blamphin's ballad *Little Maggie May* differs significantly in form to the later sea shanty *Maggie May* it does contain some similar themes such as '*Down by a Little running brook I first saw Maggie May*", which mirrors the line 'W*hen I first saw Maggie May, she was cruising up and down…*' oft contained in versions of the latter song, and it of course refers to '*Maggie, Maggie May*' as does the latter song. Interestingly it also refers to her '*singing all the day*', as does *Nelly Ray* the ode to a Kent farmer's daughter popularised in the Music Halls just a few years later.

Victorian era Broadsheet of *Little Maggie May*

George Washington *'Pony'* Moore (*1820-1909)* in Minstrel costume and make up

Perhaps crucially at least one newspaper report, from Xmas Eve 1902, in Tasmania, provides evidence that some versions of *Darling Nelly Gray* were by then being sung as '*Oh me, **Little** Nelly Gray, they have taken her away, an 'I'll never see me darlin' anymore'*. It is then no great stretch to imagine *Little Nelly Gray* later morphing into *Little Maggie May* and similarly supplanting *Charming Nelly Ray* as the protagonist of the sailor's parody of the same song by 1913, particularly once the Music Halls had gone into decline and the original standards themselves were no longer regularly heard and were starting to fade in popular memory.

In conclusion, all the available evidence suggests the traditional sea shanty *Maggie May*, as we know it, was a product of the Minstrel era in England, composed as *Charming Nelly Ray* a dark parody of *Darling Nelly Gray*, possibly by music hall comics or by their rowdy dockside audiences in the early 1870s, and later added to, shaped and popularised by sailors in busy ports such as London and Liverpool, in subsequent decades. In the early 20th century it remained a song confined to below decks, naval dock yards and pub sing-a-longs, deemed unsuitable for wider publication or distribution due to its risqué content, until later revived and popularised in the 1950s by the English folk song movement and the Skiffle generation. It was then immortalised by Liverpool's most famous sons, The Beatles, on their last album *Let it Be* in 1970.

[154]

Maggie May – Version 1

As Sung by Geoff Ling at *The Ship Inn* in Blaxhall on October 10th, 1953

Now come all you soldiers bold, come listen to my plea
When you've heard my tale, you'll pity me.
For I was a darned damn fool at the port of Liverpool
The first time that I came home on leave.

I was paid off at the hold with the boys of Merrybold
Three-pound-ten a week was all my pay.
When she mingled with my tin I was very much taken in
By a little girl whose name was Maggie May.

Too well do I remember when I first met Maggie May
She was cruising up and down old Canning Town.
Oh she wore her clothes divine, like a figure on the line
So I being a soldier I gave chase.

In the morning I awoke with my heart all sore and broke
No trousers, jacket, waistcoat could I find.
When I asked her where they were,
She said to me, *"Kind sir,*
They're down in Stanley's pawnshop, number nine!"

To the pawnshop I did go no trousers,
Jacket, waistcoat could I find
And a policeman came and took that girl away.
Oh she robbed so many a sailor and many a Yankee whaler
She won't walk down Lime Street anymore.

Oh Maggie, Maggie May, they have taken her away
To slave like a n__r in the corner of Berkley Square.
The judge he guilty found her
For robbing a homeward bounder
And he paid her passage back to Monte Bay.

This early recorded example of the song as transmitted in England in the oral tradition is quite interesting for a couple of reasons. First for the line "*I was paid off at the hold, with the boys of Merrybold*" which makes little sense but might suggest in the original it appeared as '*I was paid off at the home, with the boys of Marylebone*'. The comic Andrew Edgar Wilding, was a resident of Marylebone when he introduced '*Nelly Ray*' in his act, living there from the time of his marriage in 1859, until the time of his divorce in 1876. Secondly the line '*She was cruising up and down old Canning Town*', could also support the theory the song was originally composed in a London setting, rather than a Liverpool one, perhaps specifically crafted by Wilding to suit his Limehouse audience (*though Ling also later refers to Lime Street*). Thirdly the line '*For she wore her clothes divine, Like a figure on the line*' may suggest the references to crinoline net frigates contained in Charles Picknell version, were later additions peculiar to some orally transmitted versions, but not to all.

[155]

Maggie May – Version 2

Sung by A.L. Lloyd on 1956 Riverside album *English Drinking Songs*

Now come all you young sailors and listen to me plea
And when you've heard me tale, you'll pity me
For I was a goddam fool in the port of Liverpool
The very first time I came home from sea

Now, I was paid off at the Home, from the port of Sierra Leone
Three-pound-ten a month it was me pay
Well, I wasted all me tin whilst drinking up the gin
With a little girl whose name was Maggie May

Now well do I remember where I first met Maggie May
She was cruising up and down in Canning Place
She was dressed up mighty fine, like a frigate of the line
So being a ranting sailor I gave chase

I kept right on her a track, she went on the other tack
But I caught her and I broke her mizzen line
Next morning I awoke with a head more bent then broke
No coat, no vest, no trousers could I find

I asked her where they were, she said – *"Me good kind sir*
They're down at Kelly's pawnshop, number nine
Now, you've had your cake and bun, and it's time for you to run
Or you'll never make the dockside, lad, in time!"

To the pawnshop I did go but no trousers could I find
And the policeman came and took that girl away
And the judge he guilty found her, of robbing a homeward-bounder
and now she's doing time in Botany Bay

Oh Maggie, Maggie May, they have taken you away
Never more to roam again down Canning Place
For you've you robbed too many whalers, and you've dosed so many sailors
And you'll never see old Lime Street anymore.

[156]

Maggie May – Version 3

As recorded in 1961 by Stan Hugill

Come all ye sailors bold
And when me tale is told
I know you all will sadly pity me,
For I was a bloomin' fool
In the port of Liverpool
On the voyage when I first paid off from sea.

I was paid off at the home for a voyage to Sierra Leone,
Two pounds ten a month had been me pay
While jingling me tin I was sadly taken in
By a lady by the name of Maggie May.

When I sailed into her I didn't have a care
She was cruising up and down old Canning Place
Dressed in a gown so fine like a frigate of the line
And me being a sailor gave her chase.

Ah me Maggie Maggie May
They've taken you away
You'll slave upon Van Diemen's cruel shore
You robbed many a sailor many a drunken whaler
But you'll never cruise down Paradise Street no more.

Next day when I awoke I found that I was broke
I didn't have a penny to me name
I had to hock me suit, me *"John L's"* and me boots
Down in the parkway pawnshop number 9.

She was chained and sent away from Liverpool one day
The lads did cheer as she sailed down the bay
And every sailor lad, he only was too glad
That they sent the old thing off to Botany Bay

Ah me Maggie Maggie May they have taken you away
And you'll slave upon Van Dieman's cruel shore
You've robbed many a sailor, many a drunken whaler
But you'll never cruise down Paradise Street no more.

[157]

Though Maggie May and her forerunner Nelly Ray were almost certainly fictional inventions, several cases found in Liverpool Newspapers 1830-1870 mirror the details of the famous song in many respects, and stand testament to the fact it was a hypothetical scenario very much with a basis in real life events:

- *31 January 1834 - Liverpool Mercury* - Mary Johnson, a disorderly woman, was charged before the Mayor, on Thursday week, with robbing a sailor of his jacket, in a house of ill fame, in Atherton-street. The prisoner restored his jacket and was discharged.

- *05 September 1837 - Liverpool Mail*- Catherine Murphy was charged with robbing a sailor of £l 18s. together with the whole of his clothes. It appeared that prosecutor met the prisoner on the preceding evening and they agreed to pass the evening together. In the morning when he awoke he found that his companion, clothes, and money had disappeared. He immediately sallied forth as he was in quest of some of the missing articles, and having met a person calling herself the landlady, he was directed to a room in the lower part of the house, where he found his clothes, minus the £l 18s. which he had in his jacket.

- *20 June 1846 - Liverpool Mail*- Two prostitutes, named Ann Johnson and Mary Bell, were, yesterday, committed for one month, on charge of robbing a sailor of his wearing apparel, in Hatton-garden, on the previous night

- *25 December 1847 - Liverpool Mail* - Yesterday, a female, named Elizabeth Bonce, who lives in a brothel in Preston street, was brought before Mr. Kushton, at the Police-court, charged with having robbed a sailor, named Poole, of thirty-eight shillings and his clothes. It appeared that Poole went with the prisoner to the house in question the previous evening and in the morning found that he had been robbed of his clothes and money. It was proved that the prisoner had pledged part of the prosecutor's clothes, and she was ordered to pay a penalty of 1 pound and five shillings, and in default of payment was committed to prison for three months.

- *21 October 1853 - Liverpool Mercury* - Ann Connor was brought up on a remand from gaol, charged with robbing a sailor named Rourke of 4 pounds 1 shilling, in a brothel in Banastre-street.

- *29 November 1853 - Liverpool Mercury* - Margaret Robinson, was charged with robbing William Brown, a sailor, of two pounds and ten shillings, six pence, and pawning his coat, in a disreputable house in Preston-street.

- *26 March 1856 - Liverpool Daily Post* - Catherine McGonnell, and Ann Conolly were indicted for robbing a sailor named James Thompson, in a house in Peter-street, on the night of the 11th instant.

- *10 July 1857 - Liverpool Mercury* - Mary O'Donnell, Emma Hughes, and Margaret Rowlande, remanded from this day a week ago for robbing a sailor, named John Daglish, of his watch, and 19 shillings at Peter Street were again brought up, and there not being sufficient evidence, discharged.

- *13 November 1865 - Liverpool Mercury* - Robbing a Drunken Sailor. — Benjamin Block, seaman, who has recently come off voyage, spending the proceeds in the sailor's usual liberal manner, charged James Williams and Ann Daley with robbing him. The prosecutor was drinking at the Lighthouse, Hanover-street, Friday afternoon, where he met with the prisoners. He treated the female to several glasses of spirits, and drank pretty freely himself. When about to pay for some drink which had been ordered, the male prisoner made a snatch for the money which the prosecutor held in his hand, and succeeded in obtaining from him half a crown.

- *15 June 1867 - Liverpool Daily Post* - Bridget Wheelan, an evil one, was brought up on remand charged with having robbed Christopher Byrne, a, sailor, of £5 note and £2 in gold. —On the previous occasion she stated that she had not seen the £2, but the £5 note she had given Henry Dodd, a barman with Mr. Kittshaw, a publican in Park-lane, to keep for her. The barman, however, on oath, said that he never received the £5 note, and a police officer was sent to the house to search for the note, the prisoner, Wheelan, being remanded until the following day was now brought up on a charge of stealing it

- *21 March 1868 - Liverpool Daily Post* - Two vile women were brought before the court in custody charged with having robbed a sailor, a remarkable looking man, in as much he exhibited altitude of little less than seven feet. The case possessed none but the usual features of such class of cases, and the prisoners were remanded.

The Liverpool Sailor's Home, Canning Place, circa 1860.

Church Street, Liverpool, 1880s

[160]

Bibliography

The Beatles - Hunter Davies (*W. W. Norton & Co*)

Lennon: The Definitive Biography - Ray Coleman (*Sidgwick & Jackson*)

John - Cynthia Lennon (*Hodder*)

Daddy Come Home - Pauline Lennon (*Angus & Robertson*)

Charlie Lennon: Uncle to A Beatle - Scott Wheeler (*Outskirts Press*)

The Quiet One, a Life of George Harrison - Alan Clayson (*Sidgwick & Jackson*)

Thank U Very Much: Mike McCartney's Family Album - Mike McCartney (*LBS*)

Imagine This: Growing up with my brother John Lennon - Julia Baird (*Hodder & Stoughton*)

Fab: An Intimate Life of Paul McCartney - Howard Sounes (*Harper & Collins*)

Up the Beatles' Family Tree - Cecil R Humphrey-Smith (*Achievements Ltd*)

The McCartney's in the town they were Born - Kevin Roach (*Trinity Mirror North West*)

Lennon's Liverpool in my life - Bill Harry (*Trinity Mirror North West*)

The Beatles Liverpool Landscapes - David Lewis (*DB Publishing*)

"I am the Beatle's nearest relative in Ireland" - (Interview by Maeve Quigley with Peter Mohan of County Monaghan, *Sunday Mirror, Jun 9, 2002*)

http://brakn.com/Jack1.html Michael Byron's website of John Lennon's ancestry.

http://triumphpc.com/mersey-beat/ Bill Harry's Mersey Beat website.

http://www.lennon.net/ Official Lennon family tree website.

ABOUT THE AUTHOR

Richard Edmunds is a writer, researcher, photographer and genealogist. He was born in Ascot, England, and was educated at Langley Grammar School, East Berkshire College, and the University of Birmingham, where he read Ancient History and Archaeology. As a writer his area of interests include music, arts, popular culture, social history and theology. He has been an active genealogist since 2006 and a Beatles fan since youth. He is also the author of **Paths of Freedom – The Bob Marley Family Tree.**

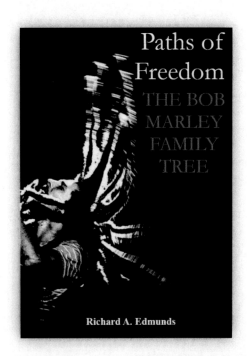

Find out more on his other works at: **www.richedmunds.co.uk**